The Hemmings Motor News Book of

HUDSONS

ISBN 0-917808-57-6
Library of Congress Card Number: 00-107813

One of a series of Hemmings Motor News Collector-Car Books. Other books in the series include:
The Hemmings Motor News Book of Cadillacs; The Hemmings Motor News Book of Chrysler Performance Cars; The Hemmings Motor News Book of Corvettes; The Hemmings Motor News Book of Mustangs; The Hemmings Motor News Book of Packards; The Hemmings Motor News Book of Pontiacs; The Hemmings Motor News Book of Postwar Fords; The Hemmings Motor News Book of Studebakers.

Hemmings Motor News
Collector Car Publications and Marketplaces
1-800-CAR-HERE (227-4373)
www.hemmings.com

The Hemmings Motor News Book of

HUDSONS

Editor-In-Chief
Terry Ehrich

Editor
Richard A. Lentinello

Designer
Nancy Bianco

Cover photo by Don Spiro

This book compiles driveReports which have appeared in *Hemmings Motor News*'s *Special Interest Autos* magazine (SIA) over the past 30 years. The editors at *Hemmings Motor News* express their gratitude to the following writers, photographers, and artists who made this book possible through their many fine contributions to *Special Interest Autos* magazine:

Jonathan Barber	Michael Lamm
Arch Brown	Ross Mac Lean
Kit Foster	Strother MacMinn
David Gooley	Alex Meredith
Ken Gross	Don Spiro
Tim Howley	Jim Tanji
Bud Juneau	Russ von Sauers
D.J. Kava	Bill Williams

We are also grateful to David Brownell, Michael Lamm, and Rich Taylor, the editors under whose guidance these driveReports were written and published. We thank American Motors Corp., Terry Boyce, BPB Publications and *Road & Track* magazine for graciously contributing photographs to *Special Interest Autos* magazine and this book.

CONTENTS

Special Interest Autos (SIA) magazine's back issues are referred to in this book by issue number. If in stock, copies may be purchased directly from Hemmings Motor News at 800-227-4373, ext. 550 or at www.hemmings.com/gifts.

1927 HUDSON SUPER-SIX

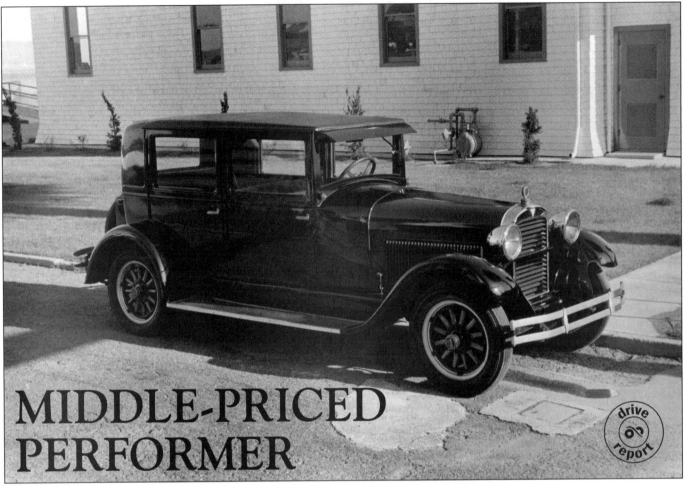

MIDDLE-PRICED PERFORMER

by Arch Brown
photos by Jim Tanji

I T was a year of transition. "Lucky Lindy's" non-stop, solo flight across the Atlantic furnished a convincing demonstration: Air travel, it was clear to anyone with eyes to see, was about to revolutionize the transportation industry.

• *The Jazz Singer*, Al Jolson's part-sound motion picture, captured the public's fancy. It wasn't the first of the "talkies." That honor had gone the year before to John Barrymore's *Don Juan*. But this one was so appealing that it spelled doom for the "silents."

• The hand-set telephone took over from the familiar, wall-mounted style.

• RCA's experimental telecast from Washington, D.C., was visible and audible in New York. What societal changes that device would bring about in a few years' time!

• Trans-Atlantic radio-telephone service was inaugurated, linking North America with the European continent.

• And Calvin Coolidge announced in his flat Yankee twang, "I do not choose to run." The Republicans would have to find another presidential candidate. Characteristically, "Silent Cal" specified no reason. His wife may have given it for him: She said her husband saw a depression coming.

Meanwhile, the automobile industry was in transition in 1927, too.

• Henry Ford was finally phasing out the ubiquitous Model T, making way for his sensational new Model A.

• Taking full advantage of the production delays occasioned by Ford's change-over, Chevrolet moved for the first time into the number one spot. They billed their 1927 model as "the most beautiful in Chevrolet history," which could have been taken as damnation by faint praise except that the car really was good-looking (see *SIA* #55).

• The eight-cylinder engine, heretofore the exclusive province of luxury cars, came to the medium-priced field. As usual it was the smaller independents that paved the way—cars like Auburn and Elcar, Gardner and Jordan. The bigger firms would follow in a few years.

Driving Impressions

When William C. Emde, a San Francisco fireman, acquired his Hudson in 1977, its speedometer had broken at 33,139 miles. There was every indication, however, that in its half-century of service it had covered no more than 40,000 miles.

Just the same, it showed the ravages of neglect. Emde bought the car from a Marin County housewife who had used it for ten years "to ferry the kids to school," as Bill puts it. Evidently the lady was somehow persuaded that old cars don't need lubricating; nor was it necessary, in her view, ever to change the oil. So, when the Hudson came home with Bill Emde its shackles were dry and both the engine and the transmission were mired in sludge. Even now the kingpins, which are original, exhibit signs of wear—wear that proper lubrication would doubtless have prevented.

Bill opened up the engine, replacing the rings and bearings, then overhauled the transmission. ("Took at least a cup of muck out of it," he reports.) The Hudson, originally blue, had been repainted in an attractive maroon, a color typical of the car's period, though not an authentic hue for this particular car. Headlining was (and is) original, though the seats had been reupholstered in a velour similar to the factory fabric. Bill installed new carpeting, then added one more cosmetic touch by refinishing the natural-spoke wooden wheels. ("Forty-eight spokes at an hour and a half apiece," he recalls.)

We encountered a familiar problem in boarding the Hudson: Though the rear-hinged "suicide" doors help a little, clearance between the door frame and the front seat wasn't designed for size twelves! There's lots of front seat leg room, however, and to the rear even a six-footer's legs can be stretched out at full length. With the help of a wrench the front seat can be moved to any one of three positions—a nuisance to adjust, but a big improvement over the fixed position that was the norm for car seats in 1927.

There is no ignition key; the car is secured by locking the transmission in neutral. There was some reluctance on the Hudson's part when we flipped the switch and jabbed the floor-mounted starter lever, but presently the engine fired. By the standards of its day it's a quiet engine, yet its sound conveys the feeling of great power—a totally accurate impression, as we were about to discover.

In typical Hudson fashion the clutch is silky-smooth, and pedal pressure is minimal. The straight-cut gears make double-clutching advisable, but shifting requires little effort. Acceleration, for a big, heavy old automobile, is remarkably brisk.

This would have been a great car for the ladies, back in the "flapper" era when it was new. Its steering, which is relatively quick, is much lighter than we anticipated, and the heavy, solid walnut wheel feels good to the hands. Similarly, the huge Bendix brakes require only gentle pressure. They do their job well in normal driving, though Bill Emde reports that under

hard use their light, pressed-steel drums give them a tendency to fade. Withal the car handles beautifully, and we can readily understand why its owner enjoys driving it.

For our photo session we took the Hudson to the Coast Guard station on the waterfront, close by the Golden Gate, and then on to San Francisco's historic US Army Presidio. The two locations adjoin each other, connected by a narrow road ascending a sharp incline. There, we put the Super-Six through its paces.

Its legendary hill-climbing ability is no myth. Starting from a dead stop at the bottom of the grade, we ran through the gears. Then, on a hill that would challenge the second-gear capability of most cars, the Hudson walked right up the incline *in high.* It was an incredible performance. One might suspect that the car drives through a stump-puller of a rear axle ratio, but in truth the '27 Hudson's gears are taller than those of any of its competitors (see sidebar, page 7). Hudson published no figures on the subject in those days, but the low-end torque, abetted no doubt by the engine's healthy five-inch stroke, is truly impressive. Bill Emde tells of taking the car to the top of Mount Tamalpias in top gear with four people aboard, a feat that few modern cars could match. And on the open road it cruises easily at freeway speeds.

No doubt the Hudson's long (127.375-inch) wheelbase contributes to its very comfortable ride. Its springs have 15 leaves apiece, providing a cushioning effect that simply isn't possible with the customary six or seven leaves. Snubbers take the place of the modern automobile's shock absorbers, with the result that the spring action is a little abrupt on hard bumps, but overall the Hudson treats its passengers very kindly. The rear springs are splayed, helping to minimize any tendency to lean on the turns.

There are some unusual conveniences to be found: A sight-gauge, utilizing a cork float, instantly shows the level of the

crankcase oil; and a handy, all-steel trunk fits between the body and the rear-mounted spare tire. On the other hand, the overhead intake valves must be lubricated by hand. Six little cups, mounted atop the engine, supply oil to the wicks, which in turn get the job of lubrication done. There is no thermostat; radiator shutters controlled by a dashboard lever to the driver's left, adjust the flow of air, thus governing engine heat.

Incidentally, the location of the spark plugs on the driver's side reveals the Emde car to have been built relatively early in the model year. Plugs in the later units were fitted to the right side, in the interest of controlling detonation. Since this problem has never surfaced in Bill Emde's experience, he concludes that the inferior fuels of 1927 were the principal source of the trouble.

Bill reports that the Hudson can become a veritable "house of mirrors" at night. Since all the glass—including the windshield—is vertical, lights from other cars bounce off one window, only to be reflected in another.

Come to think of it, our readers may have seen this car before. It appeared in the opening "trailer" used with each episode of the TV mini-series, *The Gangster Chronicles,* and it was also used in the filming of the movie *Hammett.*

It's an impressive vehicle, this Hudson. But it failed to impress the car-buying public—anyway, not in the numbers one might have expected. By year's end, Hudson's 1927 new car registrations put it in eleventh place, trailing all of its major rivals: Buick (third), Chrysler (fifth), Nash (eighth), and Studebaker (tenth). So it hardly comes as a surprise that as the decade drew to a close Hudson was preparing to replace the fabulous Super-Six with a less expensive car featuring a straight-eight version of the company's Essex engine. That one came along for the 1930 season, just in time to knock heads with the Depression. They called it the Hudson Greater Eight.

1927 HUDSON

Above: '27 Hudsons carried vastly more plating up front than previous models. **Right:** New headlight design replaced drum style seen on earlier cars. **Below:** Sidelamps are mounted on windshield frame.

1927 Hudson Body Styles, Prices, and Weights

At introduction time (January 1927) Hudson offered two body styles in the "Standard" series, five in the "Custom."

	Price	Weight
STANDARD SERIES		
Coach (118-inch wheelbase)	$1,285	3,505 pounds
Sedan (127-3/8-inch wheelbase)	$1,385	3,620 pounds
CUSTOM SERIES (all 127-3/8-inch wheelbase)		
Brougham	$1,575	3,660 pounds
Phaeton (7-passenger)	$1,600	3,565 pounds
Roadster	$1,500	N/A
Sedan (5-passenger)	$1,750	3,755 pounds
Sedan (7-passenger)	$1,850	3,870 pounds

At mid-year, two new "Standard" cars were introduced, and prices were cut on several models. New to the line were the following:

Body style	Price	Weight
Sedan (118-inch wheelbase)	$1,285	3,585 pounds
Coach (127-3/8-inch wheelbase)	$1,285	3,555 pounds

Price cuts were made as follows:

Model/body style	Old price	New price
Standard coach (118-inch wheelbase)	$1,285	$1,175
Custom phaeton	$1,600	$1,500
Custom roadster	$1,500	$1,400

• A number of the small manufacturers, no longer able to remain competitive, packed it in. Wills Ste. Claire was one of the best of these, and it had plenty of company: Rickenbacker, for instance; and before the year's end, Billy Durant's Flint. Others would shortly join the casualty list.

• On the other hand, there were a few newcomers to the field. John North Willys's Falcon Knight brought a sleeve-valve six to the thousand-dollar field in March, though the public was clearly underwhelmed, and Reo fielded its new Wolverine a few weeks later. Dodge Brothers introduced its first six; so did Durant's Star. And the Graham brothers bought control of Paige-Detroit, although the car that would bear their name wouldn't appear for another year.

• Billy Durant, meanwhile, was making the rounds of independent motorcar manufacturers in an effort to put together a combine which he hopefully entitled "Consolidated Motors." But Billy had lost his magic touch, and he could find no takers. His own empire was falling apart: The Durant was dead, though the name would be revived the following year; the Flint was dying; Locomobile was on the ropes; and Billy's Star wasn't shining all that brightly, either.

• Studebaker and Jordan were attempting to launch "compact" cars, though George Romney wouldn't coin the term for another quarter-century. They bombed, both of them. Ned Jordan's flashy "Little Custom" was a competent and very stylish automobile, cute as a bug, but it sold for more money than a Chrysler 70, and the public simply couldn't see it. Studebaker's junior edition, which company president Albert Erskine modestly named for himself, was another matter. It didn't require a mechanical genius to figure out that the Erskine's ultra-long-stroke, 146-cubic-inch Continental engine, driving through a 5.1:1 axle, would soon pound itself to bits—which is exactly what it did.

• Taking timely advantage of Henry Ford's extended shutdown, John Willys came up with the peppy, economical 30-horsepower Whippet (see *SIA* #66). Another "compact" it was, and this one succeeded—for a time. By 1928 it held fourth place in the industry, in fact, though two years later it would plummet ignominiously to twentieth rank.

If Hudson wasn't exactly in transition in 1927, at least it had a brand new car to show. A little more expensive than the 1926 model, it was completely restyled,

Left: "Suicide" style doors both front and rear offer easy access to Hudson's interior. *Below:* Out back, an accessory trunk of the period solves the luggage carrying question on driveReport car.

with smoother lines and more rounded contours. Unlike its boxy predecessor, Hudson's 1927 car was rather a handsome piece of equipage.

It was also an exceedingly competent performer. Ever since the introduction of the first Super-Six, back in 1916, Hudson had racked up record after record in competitive events: In hillclimbs, on the racetrack, and on crosscountry dashes, no car at the Hudson's price (and few at any price) could match the collection of trophies amassed by the Super-Six.

But now, a new engine powered the Hudson. Though it retained the historic 3-1/2-inch x 5-Inch dimensions initiated by Hudson more than a decade earlier, it had been converted from "L-head" to "F-head" configuration, with huge intake valves fitted to the cylinder head. The improved breathing that resulted from this change, together with a higher compression ratio, an improved ignition system, and a new method of carburetion, provided a startling 25 per-

1927 Hudson Versus Its Competition: A Comparison Table

Make	Price*	Cyls.	Valves	C.I.D.	Hp/rpm	Lubric. System	Steering	Axle Ratio	Brakes	Tires	Curb Weight	Wheelbase
Hudson	$1,285	6	F-head	288.6	95/3,100	Splash	Worm & sector	4.08:1	Mech.	31x6.00	3,505	118"
Buick 115	$1,195	6	In-hd.	207.0	63/2,800	Press.	Worm & nut	4.90:1	Mech.	31x5.75	3,150	114.5"
Buick 120	$1,395	6	In-hd.	274.0	77/2,800	Press.	Worm & nut	4.51:1	Mech.	33x6.00	3,670	120"
Chrysler 60	$1,145	6	L-head	180.4	54/3000	Press.	Cam & lever	4.60:1	Hydr.	28x5.25	2,795	109"
Chrysler 70	$1,525	6	L-head	218.5	70/3,000	Press.	Worm & sector	4.30:1	Hydr.	30x6.00	3,090	112.75"
Nash Special	$1,215	6	In-hd.	224.0	52/2,600	Press.	Worm & sector	4.89:1	Mech.	31x5.25	3,150	112.5"
Nash Advanced	$1,425	6	In-hd.	278.4	69/2,500	Press.	Worm & roller	4.50:1	Mech.	33x6.00	3,550	121"
Peerless 6-80	$1,395	6	L-head	230.2	63/2,600	Press.	Cam & lever	4.45:1	Hydr.	32x6.00	3,100	116"
Studebaker Standard	$1,230	6	L-head	242.0	50/2,200	Press.	Worm & wheel	4.18:1	Mech.	31x5.25	3,210	113"
Studebaker Special	$1,480	6	L-head	289.0	65/2,400	Press.	Worm & wheel	4.36:1	Mech.	32x6.00	3,470	120"

Note that among the Hudson's competitors, only those models costing substantially more than the Super-Six were comparable to it in terms of size and weight—and none was really comparable in power.

Sources: *Automotive Industries*, February 19, 1927; *MoToR*, January 1927.

Prices, weights, wheelbases shown are for the lowest-priced, five-passenger closed body style.

1927 HUDSON

Above: Hudson's famous triangle motif appears on the cast-aluminum hubcaps. *Right:* Grease cups on rear spring shackles were becoming an antiquated method of chassis lubrication by 1927.

cent increase in power output. At 95 horsepower it was by far the most powerful car in its price class (see sidebar, page 7). The factory boasted of a top speed of 102 miles an hour in a test run by a strictly stock unit (though some Hudson authorities today consider the claim to be suspect), while a "constant road speed" of 70 was "guaranteed." Few cars in 1927 could match that, whatever their price; certainly none at the Hudson's comparatively modest tab of $1,285.

Hudson's copy-writers grew ecstatic. "The smoothness with which the Super-Six glides from standing start to high speed is totally different from the violent lunge with which high-powered cars usually get under way," declared one ad—intended, no doubt, to reassure the ladies that the Hudson was as docile as it was quick. Describing the new Super-Six as "the most talked-of car of the year," another Hudson advertisement declared, "The Super-Six has the smoothness of an electric motor. Four years' development led to full release of its capacity in power, stamina, and safety. From the effortless smoothness with which the Super-Six whisks you into motion, to the carefree way in which you may make any trip from a journey downtown to a run across the continent, there remains throughout the zest of driving that is possible only

Essex: The Tail that Wagged The Dog

If its senior line represented the Hudson Motor Car Company's engineering tour de force in 1927, it was the moderately priced Essex that provided the corporate bread-and-butter. For the smaller car outsold its big brother by a margin of nearly three to one.

The introduction in 1922 of the Hudson coach, with its dramatic effect upon the cost of closed-bodied automobiles in the medium-priced field, had its parallel in the Essex among moderately priced cars. By 1924 the spread between closed and open Essex cars had narrowed to $125, compared to a $355 differential in the case of the Dodge, and even more in certain other instances. (Durant, for example, charged a stiff $475 premium for its cheapest sedan model.)

And a year later the Essex coach cost five dollars less than the touring car, a reversal without parallel in the industry at that time—except, of course, for the Hudson.

By 1927 the Essex had elbowed Dodge aside to take over fourth place in US car sales, behind Chevrolet, Ford, and Buick. Partly it was the momentum of the highly successful coach, for Hudson and Essex were still the only automobiles to make a closed body available at a lower price than an open-style car. But by that time the premium charged by the competition for the comfort of a closed car had been sharply reduced, generally to about $100—and to a mere $30 in the case of the Chrysler 50.

The principal factor in the surging popularity of the Essex during the mid-twenties, however, was undoubtedly the introduction in 1924 of its first six. Priced in coach form at least $100 below the six-cylinder offerings of any other manufacturer, it had been an instant success.

Strictly speaking, incidentally, the Essex could not at that time be considered a "low-priced" car. With prices beginning at $850, it cost $45 less than a Dodge, $500 less than a Hudson, but the tab was, nevertheless, $355 more than that of a Chevrolet.

There were still a number of medium-priced fours on the market in 1924, and even a couple of sophisticated four-bangers in the high-priced range, but their days were numbered. Buick and Nash would replace their four-cylinder cars with sixes the following year; Auburn and Oldsmobile already built sixes exclusively. So the motoring public was quite literally waiting for a six-cylinder car that the average family could afford.

When 1927 rolled around, the Essex—besides costing less than fours from Chrysler and Dodge—was by any measure the industry's lowest-priced six. But the margin, vis-a-vis the competition, was shrinking. The new, six-cylinder version of John North Willys's highly successful Overland Whippet was priced only $60 above the Essex, and GM's Pontiac fetched just $30 more than the Whippet.

Of course, that first six-cylinder Essex, with its 129.9-cubic-inch engine, had been a pretty anemic automobile—and not a very durable one, either. But by 1927 the little mill had been bored and stroked to 144.7 cubes and some of its inherent weaknesses, especially in the splash oiling system, had been remedied. Smooth new styling paralleled that of the Hudson, and if the Essex's brakes still functioned only on the rear wheels—well, so did those of the Pontiac!

If 1927 was, in Frank Sinatra's phrase, "a very good year" for Hudson—and it was; the company's share of the market rose by 39 percent over 1926—credit the Essex with most of the gain. But in truth 1927 was no more than a prelude. By 1929 the Essex would take its place, if only briefly, as the industry's number-three nameplate.

specifications

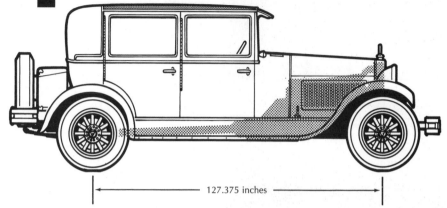

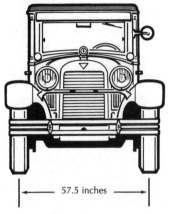

127.375 inches

57.5 inches

1927 Hudson Super-Six

Price	$1,385 f.o.b. factory, with standard equipment
Standard equipment	"Automatic" windshield wiper, rear view mirror, shutters, Boyce Moto-Meter, fuel gauge on dash

ENGINE

Type	6-cylinder, F-head, cast en bloc
Bore x stroke	3.5 inches x 5 inches
Displacement	288.6 cubic inches
Max bhp @ rpm	95 @ 3,100
Max torque @ rpm	N/a
Compression ratio	N/a. Believed to be about 5.5:1
Induction system	Marvel 1.5" updraft carburetor; vacuum feed
Lubrication system	Splash
Electrical system	Auto-Lite, 6-volt
Number main brgs	4
Valve lifters	Hydraulic

CLUTCH

Type	Single-plate, cork inserts
Diameter	12 inches
Actuation	Mechanical, foot pedal

TRANSMISSION

Type	3-speed selective sliding gear (Hudson-built)

Ratios:	1st	3.04:1
	2nd	1.81:1
	3rd	Direct
	Reverse	3.69:1

DIFFERENTIAL

Type	Spiral bevel
Ratio	4.08:1
Drive axles	Semi-floating

STEERING

Type	Gemmer worm-and-sector
Turns, lock-to-lock	3
Ratio	11.5:1
Turning circle	49 feet (wall-to-wall)

BRAKES

Type	Bendix internal four-wheel mechanical
Drum diameter	14 inches
Total braking area	305 square inches

CHASSIS & BODY

Frame	Ladder-type, 6 cross members
Body construction	Steel
Body style	5-passenger sedan
Body manufacturer	Briggs

SUSPENSION

Front	Semi-elliptical longitudinal leaf springs
Rear	Semi-elliptical longitudinal leaf springs
Tires	31 x 6.00
Wheels	18-inch wooden artillery-type

WEIGHTS AND MEASURES

Wheelbase	127.375 inches
Overall length	186 inches
Overall height	76 inches
Overall width	68 inches
Front tread	57.5 inches
Rear tread	56.5 inches
Ground clearance	9 inches
Curb weight	3,620 pounds

CAPACITIES

Crankcase	9 quarts
Cooling system	16 quarts
Fuel tank	18.75 gallons

PERFORMANCE

(factory claims)

Cruising speed	70 miles per hour
Fuel consumption	17-18 miles per gallon

Updraft Marvel carburetor feeds the big F-head six.

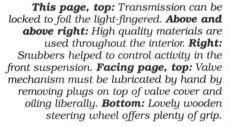

This page, top: Transmission can be locked to foil the light-fingered. **Above and above right:** High quality materials are used throughout the interior. **Right:** Snubbers helped to control activity in the front suspension. **Facing page, top:** Valve mechanism must be lubricated by hand by removing plugs on top of valve cover and oiling liberally. **Bottom:** Lovely wooden steering wheel offers plenty of grip.

to its elastic and smooth flow of power."

Nor were the Hudson's improvements confined to its engine. For the first time in the company's history, four-wheel brakes were employed, and in another move that had styling as well as safety implications, the center of gravity was lowered by some four inches. A single-plate clutch replaced the earlier multiple-disc type (though Hudson's traditional cork inserts were retained); the parking brake was moved to the left, out of the way of the passengers' feet; and an automatic spark advance was adopted. The radiator's cooling surface was increased by 16 percent, and a 50 percent hotter spark was claimed for the revised ignition system.

Two distinct lines of bodies were offered, though their styling was nearly identical. The Standard line was of steel construction, and consisted initially of a coach, built on a 118-inch wheelbase, and a four-window sedan on a 127-inch chassis. (Our driveReport car is a prime example of the latter.) At mid-year two new styles were offered, a six-window sedan on the shorter chassis and a long-wheelbase coach. Bodies for the long-wheelbase Standard cars came from Briggs, while Hudson did its own coachwork for the shorter models.

The Custom series, all of which came on the 127-inch chassis, was very nearly

"The Hairy Hudson"

After having sampled the fabulous performance of Bill Emde's Super-Six, we were interested in learning more about Hudson's remarkable record, over the years, in competitive events. We learned that Alex Burr, of Kennebunk, Maine, has compiled a substantial file on the subject, so we wrote to Alex. Mentioning this driveReport, we asked him to share some Hudson highlights with *SIA* readers.

The following is excerpted from his reply.

"The Hudson Motor Car Company literally hit the ground running, back in 1909-1910. During the 1910 season Hudson's little four-cylinder wonder set many and varied records all across the country, from Richmond, Virginia, to Seattle, Washington — usually winning whatever event it was entered in.

"No doubt there was racing activity between 1911 and 1915, but I have nothing in my files. With the introduction of the famous 'Super-Six' in December 1915, however, Hudson was really in the racing game. Even before its introduction to the motoring public, one of these cars set a record of 80 minutes, 21.4 seconds over a 100-mile course at Sheepshead Bay, Long Island, for an average speed of 74.9 miles an hour.

"1916 was an eventful year. Among the notable events was, of course, the famous transcontinental run. Not satisfied with breaking the San Francisco-New York record by making the traverse in five days, three hours, and 31 minutes, the crew turned around and went back to San Francisco. The total, round-trip took ten days, 21 hours, three minutes.

"Stepping back a bit to August 12, 1916, during the first of the great Pike's Peak hill-climbing events, Ralph Mulford took a 'Super-Six' to the top in 18:24.7, setting a record for the under-300 c.i.d. class. A Denver newspaper observed that there were 'Fours, Sixes, Eights, Twelves, and Super-Sixes.' And on April 10th of that year was the AAA outing at Daytona Beach. There, Mulford set a 12-hour mark of 912 miles and then went on to shatter the 24-hour record by covering 1,819 miles. During this run he set a new stock mile record, officially timed by the AAA at 102.5 miles an hour.

"So the 1927 Hudson has, as you can see, quite a heritage. Once again, there isn't much in my files dealing with the 1920s. About all I have is a note telling that on the day Lindbergh landed in Paris, May 21, 1927, Barney Oldfield pushed a stock 1927 Hudson to a new world's record for 1,000 miles on the Culver City

(California) board track. I have no other details of that event.

"What it all comes down to, I think, is that Hudson engineers consistently underrated their engines. There is an unsubstantiated story that in the 1950s, when Hudsons were running the wheels off the competition on the stock car tracks, Hudson engineers got their hands on some of the other companies' engines and ran dynamometer tests on them. Their findings came out consistently lower than the figures attributed to those engines. Come to find out, so the story goes, everybody in Detroit was testing for horsepower with 'bare' blocks — no generators, no water pumps, nothing that would cause drag and cut down the power. Hudson was testing theirs with all components in place, and getting — with the 1951-52 Hornet engines — around 145 horsepower. And later, 170 with the cast-iron head, 175 with aluminum, out of the 1954s. Knowing Hudson, the story may not be as far-fetched as it sounds. Of course, the secret of the 1951-54 Hornets on the stock-car track was the 'step-down' design. The darn car was wider than it was high, and with the lower center of gravity it could go deeper into the turns at speed than the others, thus gaining a bit each lap and finally winning the race."

what the name implies, for the bodies, built of aluminum over hardwood framing, came from no less prestigious a source than Biddle and Smart. Offered were two open styles — roadster and phaeton — plus a five- and seven-passenger sedan, and a smartly styled brougham. These cars, which sold at a premium of about $350 over the Standard series, are readily distinguished by their conventional door hinges. The Standard cars continued to feature Hudson's traditional "piano" hinges — incredibly strong, but virtually impossible to repair in the event of an accident

Interiors of all closed models featured plush velour upholstery, and the dashboard instruments were grouped under a glass panel and indirectly lighted. The cluster included a fuel gauge, ammeter, and oil pressure gauge in addition to the speedometer. Engine temperature was monitored by a Boyce Moto-Meter, mounted on the radiator cap. ◌

Acknowledgements and Bibliography
Automotive Industries, *January 8, 1927, and February 19, 1927; John A. Conde,* The Cars That Hudson Built*; Maurice D. Hendry, "Hudson, the Car Named for Jackson's Wife's Uncle,"* Automobile Quarterly, *Vol. IX, No. 4; Beverly Rae Kimes, "It Was a Very Good Year. 1927,"* Automobile Quarterly, *Vol. XIV, No. 3; Julius Mattfield,* Variety Music Cavalcade*; Ted W. Mayborn (archivist),* Hudson; The Story of the Hudson Motor Car, 1909-1957; MoToR, *January 1927;* Automobile Trade Journal, *January 1927.*
Our thanks to Dave Brown, Durham, California; Alex Burr, Kennebunk, Maine; Evo Cuelho, Brentwood, California; Ralph Dunwoodie, Sun Valley, Nevada; D.J Kava, Beaumont, Texas. Special thanks to William C. Emde, San Francisco, California.

"The Hudson Revolution"

If Ford can be credited with bringing automobile prices within the reach of the average American family, it was Hudson that was responsible for forcing the rapid drop in the price of closed cars which occurred in the early to mid twenties.

Hudsons were not inexpensive in those days. The company's touring cars — the most popular of all body styles then — typically sold at a premium of more than $100 over the price of a comparable Buick or Nash Six. But when Hudson introduced its first coach (the then-current name for a two-door sedan) in 1922, it undercut the competition's closed cars by several hundred dollars. And that was only the beginning. Over a five-year period Hudson steadily reduced its own prices while its competitors scrambled to keep up — and never quite succeeded. The following table tells the story.

(Prices shown are for the least expensive four- or five-passenger closed model):

Year	Hudson	Buick	Nash
1922	$1,795	$2,195	$2,090
1923	$1,375	$1,895	$1,890
1924	$1,345	$1,695	$1,640
1925	$1,165	$1,495	$1,485
1926	$1,095	$1,395	$1,425

1929 Hudson Sport Phaeton

Middle Class Classic

by Kit Foster
photos by the author

Nineteen twenty-nine was a very good year. For the Hudson Motor Car Company, it was an *extraordinary* year: Their lower-priced "companion" make, Essex, rolled out shipments of 227,653 cars, making it the third-best-selling automotive label in the country, the best showing by an independent manufacturer ever (or since), and the parent Hudson produced over 70,000 cars, an effort previously bested only in 1925, when over 100,000 were sold. The 1929 cars reached a pinnacle, too, certainly in size and arguably in style. Many regard the 1929 long-wheelbase Model L as a Hudson apart from all others. Certainly this is the case at the Classic Car Club of America, where the "L" is the only Hudson accorded Classic status without special application.

The birth of Hudson has been recounted sufficiently often that we won't belabor it here. The car's namesake was none of the four ex-Olds employees, Roy Chapin, Roscoe Jackson, Howard Coffin, and George Dunham, who collaborated on the first car. The name Hudson, rather, represented the money behind the venture — put up by Detroit department store magnate Joseph L. Hudson, the uncle, incidentally, of Jackson's wife.

That first car, the Hudson Model Twenty, was a four-cylinder roadster of, appropriately, 20 bhp and 100-inch wheelbase. Designed by Dunham, it sold for $900, the modest price being a tenet of Chapin's. Rising costs, however, forced ascension to a $1,000 tag within a few months.

By August 1912, the firm had entered the six-cylinder market, heretofore the province of the automotive upper crust. The Model 54, again so named because of its horsepower, had an L-head engine configured in two blocks of three on a common crankcase. It displaced a whopping 420 cubic inches. Its oil-filled cork clutch, of the type introduced on the 1911 Model 33 and which would be a Hudson trademark until 1954, was mounted in unit with the engine. The company had begun to advertise itself as the "World's Largest Builder of Six-Cylinder Cars" on the strength of the 54, which, though nearly as large and

Driving Impressions

Ed Moore, of Bellingham, Massachusetts, literally grew up with Hudsons. When his father Donald finally gave up on his Playboy franchise (see "The Playboys Are Back in Town," *SIA* #120), he took on a Hudson dealership, and stayed with that make right through into the Rambler era. Ed collects all sorts of autos, and for many years specialized in Nash-Healeys, but given his heritage it's no surprise that he was eventually drawn back to Hudson. And what better automobile to have than the 1929 Sport Phaeton, the car considered by many to be the ultimate Hudson.

There weren't many of them in their own day, and there are fewer around now. It took Ed a couple of years from the time he made the decision to buy one until a car came on the market and he was able to close a deal. His car came from a Midwestern collector and had been carefully restored some years before. It's still a knockout, both from a distance and up close, though it has a few individual touches that might rankle purists. The radiator screen, for example, felt by some to be almost *de rigueur* for classics, is nothing ever offered by Hudson, and it further masks the car's personality by obscuring the distinctive Hudson shuttered radiator. I'd remove it, but Ed isn't sure. The hubcaps are not the proper 1929 item, having come, reportedly, from Roy Chapin's own seven-passenger limo. The former owner liked them better, and Ed tends to agree, so they remain, at least for

the moment. The flying lady radiator ornament should properly grace the cap of a 1928 Hudson; it was gone from the Hudson parts list by 1929, but many '29 owners like its style. You can see it in *some* of our photos, but since Ed also has a standard plain cap, originality is only a few threads away.

The Sport Phaeton *looks* every bit a Classic, its 139-inch wheelbase supplying the requisite lankiness, and the dual cowl and passenger windshield furnish an additional dollop of cachet. The driver's perch gives the expected tunnel view down the long hood, and the appointments bespeak quality if not lavishness. One associates Classics with whisper-smooth eight-, twelve-, or sixteen-cylinder engines. It somewhat breaks the spell, then, when the car opens its mouth, so to speak. As Professor 'enry 'iggins grimaced at the Cockney tones of Eliza Doolittle, so I recognized the same Auto-Lite starter and six-cylinder roar that accompany the firing-up of my own 1925 Hudson Brougham. Even the gear whine is the same, though there's a bit more clatter from the engine, probably a result of the overhead intake valves. But perhaps instead of experiencing disappointment I should have appreciated the fact that though this girl had moved uptown, she had not become ashamed of her solid mid-American roots.

Entry is hindered a bit by the left-hand emergency brake, but once in there's plen-

ty of leg and foot room, at least for an average-sized person like me. In any case, the driver is treated to gobs of six-cylinder torque and, once the car is warm, can navigate most anywhere in high gear; who needs an automatic transmission? Shifting is not synchronized but takes little effort after one has learned the precise pause interval needed for silent upshifts. The Hudson fluid-filled cork clutch is legendary, and this one upheld its reputation for smoothness.

The brakes take lots of pressure, and seem a bit vague, but when one stands on them they stop the car straight and true. They would not seem so out-of-sorts, I'm sure, if we weren't all used to power discs in this day and age. The steering lets the car down, as it takes a lot of strength to maneuver, especially at slow speeds, and it seems to bind a bit, even on the open road. Ed plans to give the kingpins some attention, and I'm sure that will help a lot, if my experience with other Hudsons is any gauge.

So, what's it like for the folks in the rear? Cozy. The tonneau lifts easily on counterbalanced hinges and, once it is latched back in place, gives a nice cocoon-like feeling. The rear windshield, too, does its job, for there's hardly any wind to be felt, even at speed.

Yes, this is the ultimate Hudson, its small-town accent notwithstanding. But if you want one, be patient. They don't make them any more, and they made so very few 62 years ago.

drive report

1927 Hudson

Above: Hudson's wheelbase is just one inch shorter than '29 Cadillac's; longer than the rest of the competition. *Below:* Dual sidemounts add to Classic appearance.

Comparison Table
1929 Moderately Priced Classic Phaetons

"Our feeling is," an official at the Classic Car Club of America once told this writer, "that the [Hudson] Model L 'barely qualified' for Classic status." That may be so, but it appears to have plenty of company, at least from an objective view of the data. No doubt it receives demerits for having but six cylinders, but then so does the Chrysler Imperial.

	Price	Wheelbase	Weight	Engine	C.I.D.	BHP
Hudson L	$2,200	139"	3,795 lb.	6 F hd	289	92
Studebaker President FE	$2,085	135"	4,210 lb.	8 sv	337	114
LaSalle	$2,875	125"	4,405 lb.	V-8 sv	328	85
Cadillac 341B	$3,450	140"	4,635 lb.	V-8 sv	341	90
Chrysler Imperial 80L	$3,095	136"	3,925 lb.	6 sv	310	112
Graham-Paige 837	$2,195	137"	4,405 lb.	8 sv	322	120
Kissel 8-126	$3,275	132/139"	3,990 lb.	8 sv	299	126
Packard Std. Eight	$2,385	133.5"	3,905 lb.	8 sv	319	90
Auburn 8-120	$2,095	129"	N/A	8 sv	299	120

powerful as the offerings of the "three P's," was priced more like a Studebaker.

1914 brought a smaller, lighter, and cheaper six, the Model 6-40 (40-hp, of course), a car so successful that the larger 54 was dropped as soon as its supply of parts was used up in 1916.

The big news for 1916 was the "Super Six," a name that would herald Hudson cars for over a decade and reappear periodically right into the fifties. The heart of the Super Six was a new engine, interestingly identical in displacement to the 6-40 but otherwise completely different. Designed by Charles H. Vincent, brother of Jesse Vincent of Packard Twin Six fame, it was the first engine actually built by Hudson (the earlier powerplants having come principally from Continental). It featured large valves for easy breathing, a new design camshaft, and high (for the time) compression. With bore and stroke of 3.5 by 5 inches, it displaced 288.6 cubic inches. The magic ingredient in the Super Six engine was its patented counterbalanced crankshaft, the brainchild of talented Hungarian engineer and mathematician Stephen Fekete. Fekete fitted eight counterweights to the four-main-bearing shaft, which reduced distortion, lowered friction, and permitted higher engine speeds. The Super Six delivered 70 bhp, ten more than the Cadillac V-8.

This was the age when speed and endurance records sold cars, and Hudson played the game. On September 13, 1916, Ralph Mulford set out from San Francisco with Charles Vincent and A.H. Patterson, a Stockton, California, dealer, in a new Super Six. A little over five days later the party reached New York and reversed course for the return journey. Their return to the West Coast with an overall time of 10 days, 21 hours, and three minutes for the coast-to-coast-to-coast trek set a new record, which Hudson immediately publicized as "Twice Across America." Mulford also set new records in the Super Six at Pikes Peak, for the mile at Daytona Beach, and a 24-hour mark at Sheepshead Bay, New York. In 1917, the company fielded a racing team of Mulford, Ira Vail, Billy Taylor, and Patterson, which campaigned in a fleet of tapered-tail Super Six speedsters. Hudson discontinued sponsorship of the team as the nation entered World War I, but the cars were acquired by their drivers, who continued to race them after the war.

Having established Hudson as a major force in the medium-priced market, company president Chapin turned

During the Civil War, Amesbury, Massachusetts, was a vibrant textile center, but when the market for uniforms evaporated, the local economy shifted to the abundant forests nearby. Textile mills became shops generating value-added wealth through general woodworking and carriage building. The Biddle & Smart Company of Amesbury was a successful carriage manufacturer that made the transition into automobile body production, as had many of its neighbors on "Carriage Hill." Its roots may be traced to 1869, when William Eugene Biddle, the shoe salesman son of a local baker, formed a partnership with quality carriage maker Charles H. Cadieu and purchased a wood planing mill on Water Street. Door and window frames were the first products. Biddle soon bought out his partner and embarked on making a variety of paint and wood products, including carriage parts for other manufacturers. The plant was known locally as the "Biddle Mill."

The factory was expanded, only to suffer a devastating fire in January 1876. A larger building was quickly built, and in 1880 a local carriage builder, W.W. Smart, joined the firm. Two years later they started building their own trademarked Four Hundred Buckboard. An 1883 article noted plans to build 3,000 carriages in 93 styles, from an open wagon at $490 to a $2,250 French brougham. By 1891, 270 people were employed and 4,000 carriages produced sales near $750,000. They were considered one of the "big four" carriage builders in Amesbury.

After Smart's death In 1897, finished carriage manufacturing was discontinued, and the company went back to its former role of manufacturing parts for several of the many other companies in the area.

Virtually nothing is known about the earliest auto body production, which started in 1902. Late in 1903 they were involved with the pretty Peerless limousine, which has been recognized as one of the first of this style.

Things shifted rapidly in 1905, when the death of William E. Biddle, Sr., thrust the management on his son, W.E., Jr. The younger Biddle quickly discontinued all the carriage parts business and embarked on a rapid expansion. This included the establishment of Amesbury Brass & Foundry Company, which provided hardware and accessory parts listed in the parts books. A national advertisement in *The Horseless Age* of March 15, 1905, showed the trendsetting 1904 Peerless limousine and advised: "We are Builders of Automobile Bodies of any and every description, including Limousine, Landaulets, Trucks, Delivery Wagons, Touring Cars and Runabouts. All bodies can be completely finished and upholstered in our own plant." They also offered wooden spoked wheels. One later newspaper account noted that the senior Biddle had stayed in the carriage line because he wasn't sure of the horse's demise, but one must realize that in those days total national auto production was probably less than what Amesbury itself could do in carriages. In any case, the company did well under William Junior's direction, even staying busy after the March 1907 stock market crash while some of his neighbors were idle.

By 1907, proper metal sheeting over a hardwood frame was developed as the standard construction technique. The company embarked on limited series production for a growing list of satisfied customers: touring cars for Mercer and Alco, Abbott coupes, National roadsters, Packard and Winton

Biddle and Smart
by D.J. Kava

sedans and assorted models for Lincoln, White, Chalmers, Marmon, Peerless, Haynes, Speedwell, and Club. They became specialists in using aluminum, although steel-paneled bodies were also produced.

As early as July 1914, B & S produced a series of limousines and coupes for Hudson Motor Car Company which looked "very similar to the Simplex closed cars of last year." This proved to be a fruitful association for nearly 15 years.

Before World War I, B & S owned nine buildings, including two three-story and three five-story factories, totalling approximately 300,000 square feet. As their automobile business grew, additional facilities were added by absorbing competitors or purchasing their buildings. In 1917 the largest factory in town, owned by S.R. Bailey & Co., was purchased, and a new office building was built nearby. The Auto Body & finishing Co. buildings were added in 1922. Up to 4,500 bodies a year were produced with most going to Hudson. However, local accounts recall various special one-off bodies done for com-

*Left: Interior of shop with wooden body framing set up on jigs to make '26 Hudson broughams. **Right**: Nearly completed bodies on the B & S line.*

pany executives and various movie personalities well into the 1920s.

1923 was the turning point for B & S, when the firm nearly tripled production by devoting its entire factory space to building sedans for Hudson. The big sedans sold well for a couple of years, but fashion soon shifted to the close-coupled Brougham. Production jumped to over 12,000 bodies in 1923. The plant expansion continued, B & S taking over, in the same year, the Carrier Cameron & Co. and their large "Colchester Mill" on Elm Street. In 1925 buildings from Hollander & Morrill Body Co., Witham Body Co., and T.W. Lane Company were added. The added capacity permitted acceptance of a small order from the Rolls-Royce Springfield plant. In September 1926, the Bryant Body Co. was taken over to obtain a building on Cedar Street. This brought the total space to nearly a half million square feet in 21 buildings in six different sections of town.

B & S production peaked early in 1926. In March, 400 bodies a day were produced in three eight-hour shifts by 4,736 employees. The increased production required the adaptation of the newest power woodworking tools and the use of Duco paint. These modern tools marked a move away from overhead powershafts and dangerous belts, and offered

more flexibility in arranging production space.

On the metal side, B & S used "cowl stretching," one of its more interesting advances. The company used an 18-inch-diameter Artz hydraulic ram and designed "impossible" (according to Artz) attachments to transform a flat shirt-collar-shaped piece of aluminum into an upright, beaded cowl with all the vents and necessary holes. They also worked closely with Alcoa, who would eventually supply metal which could be routinely stretched 35 to 50 percent.

After a round-the-clock operation in early 1926, "bad weather and slowness in opening of the season" slowed production considerably, but output of 40,892 bodies was still nearly a thousand more than the previous year. Also in 1926 Hudson Motor Car Company started its own body plant in Detroit to build the volume closed car coach body. It was not a good sign: by 1928 shipments would be only 40 percent of the peak years. However, the lack of a rush probably helped the customer, as the cars turned out well-built and durable.

The B & S price part lists for Hudson show series designations from B337 in 1927 to B356 in 1929, indicating at least 19 different production bodies during the three years. I have spoken with several Hudson engineers who made the overnight run to Amesbury on the train. Uniformly they described the design process as simply having B & S build suggested samples until everyone was happy.

The company also started producing its own trunks for some models. For example in January 1929 shipments show only 1,400 short-wheelbase Landau Sedans and Victoria bodies, along with 1,300 trunks. Production would have picked up during the spring, but the fact that they were making trunks instead of bodies was an ominous sign. Exact production figures for Biddle & Smart long-wheelbase 1929 bodies have so far been elusive. but estimates range up to about 800 Model L bodies, with possibly 300 of them the dual cowl Sport Phaetons.

The exact details of the corporate demise are still buried in the court records. The end probably started in December 1929, when Hudson declined to renew its usual annual contract. Even local historians have been mute on the subject, except for one vague mention of some sort of marine work. It was the second-longest surviving carriage company in Amesbury; the Walker Body Company would soon fade with the fortunes of Franklin, and completely disappear in 1933. Thus ended the heritage of the horse and carriage in Amesbury.

illustrations by Russell von Sauers, The Graphic Automobile Studio

specifications

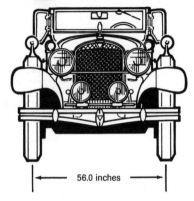

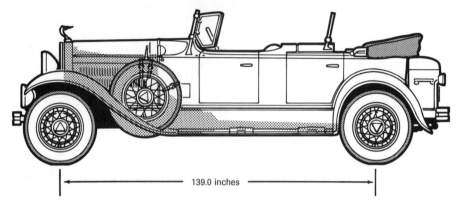

56.0 inches

139.0 inches

1929 Hudson Sport Phaeton

Price	$2,200
Standard equipment	Trico windshield wiper, wire wheels, dashboard instruments, radiator shutters, rh sidemount spare, shock absorbers, trunk rack
Optional equipment	Trunk, lh sidemount spare, driving lamps, aftermarket radiator guard

ENGINE
Type	In-line six-cylinder, cast-iron block on aluminum crankcase
Bore x stroke	3½″ x 5″
Displacement	288.6 cubic inches
Compression ratio	N/A
Horsepower @ rpm	92 @ 3,200
Taxable horsepower	29.4
Valves	Overhead intake, side exhaust (F head)
Valve lifters	Mechanical
Main bearings	4
Fuel system	1½″ Marvel updraft carburetor, Stewart vacuum tank
Cooling system	Water pump
Lubrication system	Splash with circulating pump
Exhaust system	Single
Electrical system	Auto-Lite battery/coil, 6-volt

CLUTCH
Type	Single plate, cork inserts running in oil
Diameter	13 inches
Actuation	Mechanical, foot pedal

TRANSMISSION
Type	Selective, sliding gears, 3 speeds forward, one reverse
Ratios: 1st	3.04:1
2nd	1.81:1
3rd	1.00:1
Reverse	3.69:1

DIFFERENTIAL
Type	Spiral bevel
Ratio	4⅝₂ or 4¹/₁₃ to 1
Drive axles	Semi-floating
Torque medium	Hotchkiss drive

STEERING
Type	Gemmer-roller tooth and gear variable pitch
Ratio	120:1
Turns, lock to lock	2¼
Turning diameter	20 feet

BRAKES
Type	Bendix 4-wheel mechanical, internal expanding
Drum diameter	14″
Total swept area	242 square inches

CONSTRUCTION
Type	Body on frame
Frame	Ladder frame w/channel sidemembers, 7 crossmembers

Body	Coachbuilt aluminum-over wood, steel fenders
Body style	4-passenger dual cowl sport phaeton

SUSPENSION
Front	Solid axle, longitudinal semi-elliptic springs
Rear	Live axle, longitudinal semi-elliptic springs
Wheels	Steel wire
Tires	31 x 6.50 (6.50 x 18)
Shock absorbers	Wahl double action hydraulic

WEIGHTS AND MEASURES
Wheelbase	139″
Overall length	201″
Overall width	72″
Overall height	68″ (top up)
Front track	56″
Rear track	57½ ″
Shipping weight	3,795 pounds

CAPACITIES
Crankcase	9 quarts
Fuel tank	18¼ gallons
Cooling system	5½ gallons
Transmission	1½ quarts
Differential	2½ quarts

This page: Original factory photo shows Model L phaeton sans whitewalls. *Facing page, top:* Rear cowl pulls up nearly vertical for passenger entry and exit. *Center left:* Taillamp design is typical of the times. *Center right:* Handsome factory accessory trunk looks much better than most of its contemporaries. *Bottom:* It is decidedly sportier-appearing with the top down.

1927 Hudson

his sights to the lower-priced field. Plans for the "companion" car were delayed by World War I, but the four-cylinder Essex (see *SIA* #91) debuted at the Los Angeles Auto Show on January 11, 1919. Priced at $1,395, some 70 percent of the cost of the cheapest Hudson, the Essex featured a novel overhead-intake, side-exhaust, or "F" head engine, the idea of Swiss-born engineer Emile Huber. The Essex sold 21,879 units in its first year, to the parent Hudson's 18,175. A major advance of the Essex was the two-door, four-passenger coach, the first closed car to be produced at anything like an open car price. The Briggs-bodied Essex coach, introduced in December 1921 and priced at just $1,495, $300 more than the base tourer, proved so popular that a Hudson version was made available in February of 1922.

The Super Six continued to be Hudson's staple offering into the mid-twenties. The L-head engine retained its same displacement, but incorporated many engineering advances, including a Morse silent timing chain, aluminum pistons, a new camshaft with roller tappets, and a lighter flywheel. Hudson offered a full range of bodies: a couple of phaetons, a four-passenger coupe, a four-door sedan, a limousine, and a "cabriolet," which bore handsome landau irons but did not actually convert. Curiously, there was not a roadster, but a few turtle-back speedsters had been offered from 1917 to 1919 through selected dealers. These "Walton Specials," as they were called, were bodied by the Walton Body Company of New York City.

In 1914, Hudson let their first contract for bodies to the Biddle and Smart Company of Amesbury, Massachusetts (see sidebar, page 15). At first supplying just limousines and coupes, by 1923 Biddle and Smart had become an exclusive supplier to Hudson, building five- and seven-passenger sedan bodies. The big news from Biddle and Smart for 1925 was the Brougham, a close-coupled four-door body with blind rear quarters and a leather-covered roof. The Brougham lent a bit of cachet to the Hudson line, and was an immediate success. The style was continued into 1926, and the following year was dressed up with a set of landau irons, though the leather covering on the roof was deleted. All Hudsons that year got teardrop headlamps and more rounded fenders, as the first hints of streamlining began to be applied across the board at most automobile companies. Neither Hudson nor Biddle and Smart actually had anyone on the payroll de-

scribed as a "stylist." Joseph Eskridge, retired Hudson vice president whose first job with the firm was as company representative at Biddle and Smart, recalled, when queried by historian John Conde, that the only "name" designer was Biddle and Smart's chief engineer, Arthur E. Colman.

A number of chassis changes heralded 1927 as well. The Super Six engine, still with the same bore and stroke, was converted to an F-head valve configuration with a new cylinder head, and four-wheel brakes were added. These were of the internal expanding variety, Hudson's previous binders having been the deadly-in-rain, external contracting type. The F-head was of the type used on the earlier four-cylinder Essex, and drew heavily from that experience. A number of parts in the valve train were actually the same as those from the Essex.

That same year, Hudson evidenced some further interest in the idea of styl-

ing, when the firm commissioned the Walter M. Murphy Company of Pasadena, California (see sidebar, page 18) to build a series of prototype cars using Murphy's Gangloff-inspired thin-pillar architecture. Six cars were delivered to Detroit — a landau sedan, a victoria, a seven-passenger sedan, a convertible coupe, a convertible sedan, and a fixed-head coupe — where they received an enthusiastic reception from the Hudson brass. Murphy lacked the production capability for the volume that Hudson had in mind, so the prototype cars were sent to Biddle and Smart for integration into the 1928 line. All but the convertible styles and the coupe were put into production, with minor changes, on the 1928 127.375-inch-wheelbase Model O chassis. Hudson was, by this time, building cars on two wheelbases, the smaller, more downmarket Model S at 118.5 inches.

For 1929, Hudson pulled out the stops. The entry level Model R wheel-

1927 Hudson

base grew to 122.5 inches, while the top-of-the-line Model L waded in at a whopping 139 inches, the longest to be seen on a regular production Hudson ever. Whether the firm was consciously seeking an upmarket, semi-custom clientele, or just reacting to the optimism of the age, is not clear. A hint might be found in Hudson's new name for the cars. The "Super Six" label was gone; henceforth all cars were to be called "Greater Hudsons."

The Murphy-inspired cars were carried over and split between the two series. The Victoria and the Landau Sedan were built on the Model R chassis, joining the coupe, coach, standard sedan, convertible coupe, town sedan, and a Briggs-built five-passenger

Dual Pilot-Ray driving lamps which turn with the wheels are a popular Classic-era accessory available in reproduction form today.

Frank Spring and the Murphy Connection
by Strother MacMinn

George R. Fredericks was the original general manager of the Walter M. Murphy Company, having been hired from the old Healey & Co. coachbuilders in New York, along with a cadre of craftsmen. Sometime in the early twenties, Murphy hired Frank S. Spring as an efficiency manager, surely not a popular job. On July 4, 1924, Fredericks was attending a company beach party, and responded to cries for help from a secretary who thought she was in trouble. She survived, but Fredericks drowned. Spring then became general manager. Spring and Walter M. Murphy also had a social connection: They both divorced their first wives, then married women who were sisters.

Walter Murphy's uncle William was a major investor and influence in the second Ford company (the Henry Ford Company), and brought in Henry Leland to assess the remains when Ford left. Leland recommended that they use his own engine in the Ford-designed chassis, and the result was the 1903 Cadillac. Being a friend of Leland's, William Murphy was also close to him when he began production of the Lincoln in 1922. Undoubtedly Murphy recommended his nephew Walter to be the West Coast Lincoln distributor, this in addition to Walter's having formed his coachworks in Pasadena, which could then conveniently provide proper custom bodies and, incidentally, some racy versions that would appeal to the lively Southern California clientele. The first two sport phaetons were built on Lincoln chassis; the second one was for Douglas Fairbanks, the first having been for Walter Murphy himself.

In December of 1924 Murphy swapped the Lincoln distributorship for a Hudson-Essex distributorship. Spring was then the general manager, so surely had some influence in the move. In 1927, Murphy built prototype convertible sedans for both Hudson and Auburn. The body architec-

1929 Hudson Model R landau sedan was designed by Murphy and built by Biddle and Smart.

ture was directly derived from the study of a system used by Gangloff, wherein both front and rear doors were hinged at the middle (or "B") pillar and on a common hinge line, thus allowing the glass drops to be very close together. This, in combination with cast bronze windshield pillars made as thin as possible, gave a light and airy quality to the style of the body and unimpeded visibility for the driver and passengers. This same architecture was the basis for touring sedans, hardtop sedans, and even the town car style that Murphy built on just about everything from Packard to Cord to Duesenberg.

This also reveals Spring's fascination with novel and clever ideas and accessories. He subscribed to what few there were of European publications (such as *L'Auto Carrosserie*), and that's where he discovered the Gangloff construction. He then acquired a brochure from Gangloff that showed the idea, and this very document, with his notations and diagrams in pencil, is in the W. Everett Miller Library at the Behring Museum in Danville, California.

The September 26, 1931, issue of *Automobile Topics* announced Spring's move to Hudson as "Style Engineer." He anticipated Murphy's closing by a full year, and had paved his way by having had successful business dealings with Hudson and friendship with chief engineer Stuart Baits.

I was hired by Frank Spring as a designer for Hudson, and worked there from the autumn of 1938 until the spring of 1939. As director of design, Spring made assignments and supervised the design activity, also keeping contacts with materials suppliers. He did not himself ever put pencil to paper as a hands-on designer, but did indicate what he wanted. Frank Hershey, chief designer at Murphy from 1928 to 1932 (and who would later work at GM, Hudson, and become design director at Ford) verifies this directing technique from the Murphy days. Spring might specify or indicate preference, but would not actually invent a design unless you count his participation in the discussion on how to build the Gangloff-inspired convertible sedan style.

phaeton. The seven-passenger sedan became a Model L, and a new seven-passenger limo and a club sedan were added in the Murphy slim-pillared fashion. Rounding out the Model L offering were a seven-passenger version of the Briggs phaeton and a subtly styled dual cowl Sport Phaeton built by Biddle and Smart. It is the latter car which is the subject of this driveReport, and which became the darling of Hudson fanciers many years ago.

The source of the Sport Phaeton design is not clear. Some published works have attributed it to Murphy, but Joe Eskridge who helped put the Murphy bodies into production, is less certain. "Preliminary body designs were probably made at Hudson's body engineering department for use by Biddle and Smart," he told *SIA*. "At no time then or later did I see a Murphy drawing. However, Frank Spring (Murphy's general manager and later Hudson's first 'style' engineer: see sidebar, page 18) was frequently at Hudson in 1927 and 1928. It is possible he could have shown pictures of a Murphy dual cowl phaeton on other makes of cars."

Eskridge also gives insight into the genesis of the long-wheelbase models. "The 139-inch wheelbase model for 1929 was entirely a Hudson decision," he said. "I am sure the basic body dimensions were established in Detroit and given to Biddle and Smart — probably on one-quarter-size sketches showing principal dimensions. I am sure no full-size layouts for B & S bodies were ever made in Detroit.

"My memory of work on some of the 139-inch-wheelbase models is quite clear. As an example, B & S draftsmen were having a difficult time developing the shape of the rounded trunk on the phaeton. I offered to make the full-sized draft for this trunk." The resulting trunk can be seen on our driveReport car.

Hudson prices in 1929 ranged from $1,095 for the Model R coach to $2,200 for the Sport Phaeton, both higher and lower than for comparable 1928 models. The F-head engine had been updated in mid-1927, relocating the intake valves and spark plugs to reduce detonation. Though the most obvious change was the new head, in reality this was a whole new engine: only the crankshaft interchanged with the earlier Super Six. For 1929, a new intake manifold and carburetor were introduced, and cars received self-energizing brakes and hydraulic, double-acting shock absorbers. Production soared, as has been stated, to 36 percent over that of a year earlier. Most of these were Model R's, making the L all the more exclusive by its rarity. Only 5,000 (or perhaps 3,000) are calculated to have been produced.

Above: With top up and cowl in place, rear compartment is a cozy area. *Below:* Center of steering wheel holds spark, throttle, and headlamp controls

Missing: 2,000 Hudsons

The Hudson Motor Car Company was never one to reflect on its own heritage. The firm lived for the future and not for the past, so records were often discarded. Later, during the AMC merger, a number of truckloads of remaining records went to the dump before historian John Conde made a dramatic save for latter-day researchers.

Estimates for the production of the Model L are very much a numbers game. Hudson thoughtfully assigned distinctive serial numbers to the cars, beginning, according to the late Don Butler, with 41,384. The end of the sequence is given quite authoritatively as 46,598, and as the Model R was unambiguously given numbers starting at 825,407, it would seem straightforward, by simple subtraction, to conclude that 5,214 long-wheelbase cars had been built.

Empirical evidence sometimes gives a different view. Pete Welzbacker, keeper of the 1929 register for the Hudson-Essex-Terraplane Club, lists 23 Model L cars, by serial and engine number. Interestingly,

while the lowest known existing number is 41,163 (surprise!) and the highest is 46,171, seemingly corroborating the 5,000-car estimate, there is a conspicuous gap between 41,905 and 44,090, where there are no known surviving cars. Were these "missing" cars never built, and were there therefore nearer 3,000 Model L's than 5,000? Or is this merely coincidence?

There are other uncertainties, to be sure. Earlier Hudson practice had been to allocate "blocks" of serial numbers to various body styles, but if this was done for Model L's, the blocks were quite small and were later repeated. And at least one anomaly has been discovered: a long-wheelbase club sedan in New Zealand with serial number 837,992, which should "belong" to a short-wheelbase Model R.

If you have one of these "missing" cars, or any unrecorded 1929 Hudson for that matter, contact Pete Welzbacker at PO Box 3484, Silverdale, WA 98383. You could help solve one of the remaining historical Hudson puzzles.

Above: Lockable compartments hide under tonneau cowl. *Above right:* 289-c.i.d. six develops more horses than rival Packard, Cadillac, or LaSalle. *Right:* Rear seat design is plain but posh. *Below:* It's a big, impressive automobile from any angle.

1927 Hudson

But times were changing; the events of the "Black Tuesday" stock collapse and the months that followed made that very clear. But changes had been in the wind at Hudson even before that fateful day. The 1930 models, which bowed in January, were smaller and lighter than their predecessors, with wheelbases of 119 and 126 inches. Of perhaps greater significance was the engine. Eight cylinders had become almost *de rigueur* by that time. The straight eight had been popularized by Packard in 1924 when its Twin Six was retired. In-line eights had crept into the mid-price market the following year, as nine independent manufacturers adopted them, and

Paige and Marmon introduced versions in 1927. Studebaker and Velie added eights in 1928, and Nash, DeSoto, and Dodge would join Hudson in offering such a car for 1930.

In conformance with the smaller, lighter trend, the eight was smaller than the six it replaced, at but 214 cubic inches and 80 horsepower. Hudson's engineers had designed it by the simple expediency of adding two cylinders to the lightweight Essex six, initially a troublesome powerplant, but by the late twenties cured of its shortcomings (see Essex driveReport, *SIA* #91). Bodies were restyled and were handsome, though fiscal economies resulted in sharing bodies between the Hudson and Essex lines. Prices were lower, too, beginning at $1,050

for the coach and rising to but $1,650 for the top-of-the-line seven-passenger sedan.

The "Great Eight," Hudson ads proclaimed, but the public wasn't convinced (or simply had too little money). Sales were down nearly 50 percent, and so ended, for all practical purposes, Hudson's experiment with what we would later know as the Classic era. ◌

Acknowledgments and Bibliography
Conde, John, The Cars That Hudson Built; *Butler, Don,* History of Hudson; *1922 Essex coach dR, SIA #91; Booz, Pete, and Pete Welzbacker,* "The Hudson for 1929," *White Triangle News, January-February 1989; Kostansek, Dave,* "A History of the F-head Hudson," *White Triangle News, January-February and March-April 1987; Mueller, Hans,* "Hudson a Classic? You Must Be Kidding," *Torque, July-August 1973; Hendry, Maurice,* "The Car Named for Jackson's Wife's Uncle," *Automobile Quarterly, Vol. IX, No.4; Duerksen, Menno,* "Free Wheeling," *Cars and Parts, June-August 1973; Kimes, Beverly Rae, and Henry Austin Clark, Jr.,* Standard Catalog of American Cars, 1805-1942; *Heasley, Jerry,* Production Figure Book for US Cars; *Naul, Marshall, Keith Marvin, and Stanley Yost,* Specification Book for US Cars 1920-1929; *Hudson factory literature.*

Thanks to Strother MacMinn, Pasadena, California; D.J. Kava, Beaumont, Texas; Joseph W. Eskridge, Greensboro, North Carolina; Jack Miller, Ypsilanti, Michigan; David Knowles, Sault Sainte Marie, Michigan; Pete Welzbacker, Silverdale, Washington; J. Bernard Siegfried, Liberty, Missouri; Ethan Turner and Bruce Earlin, Milford, Pennsylvania; Beverly Rae Kimes, New York, New York; Katie Robbins, Dearborn, Michigan; Richard Greene, Upper Saddle River, New Jersey; and Z. Taylor Vinson, Alexandria, Virginia. Special thanks to Ed Moore, Bellingham, Massachusetts.

THE GREATER HUDSON

The Greater Hudson Five-Passenger Sport Phaeton
92 Horsepower—above 80 miles an hour

Pride of ownership..the highest award

All motordom joins in awarding first place to the Greater Hudson, but of special significance is the way Super-Six owners everywhere lead the acclaim.

Never before was this pride of ownership so pronounced and so deserved. Thousands upon thousands, fresh from examining and driving the latest cars of the day, declare the Greater Hudson the supreme performer of their experience.

They compare its beauty, luxury and *finesse* in body detail only with the costliest cars. Throughout its brilliant performance range there is effortless ease. There is no motor labor—no sense of the mechanical. And its riding ease, they declare, is scarcely conscious of the road, whether in city travel or fast going over country highways.

64 improvements include

There are 64 improvements in the Greater Hudson and standard equipment includes: 4 hydraulic two-way shock absorbers—electric gas and oil gauge on dash—radiator shutters—double action 4-wheel brakes—saddle lamps—windshield wiper—rear view mirror—electrolock—controls on steering wheel—all bright parts chromium-plated.

The Greater Hudson is Furnished in Fourteen Body Types on Two Chassis Lengths

$1095 AND UP... AT FACTORY

Ad originally published in *The Literary Digest*, March 23, 1929

1934 HUDSON EIGHT

HUDSON COMES ROARING BACK

THE July 5, 1934, press release read: "Flash! Al Miller, driving a standard stock Hudson, broke all previous records for the spectacular and perilous Mount Washington climb this morning."

Mount Washington, for many years a favorite site for hill-climbing contests, is the highest peak in New Hampshire's Presidential Range. Rising to an altitude of 6,293 feet, the eight-mile road to the summit has been described — not altogether inaccurately — as "an unsurpassed test of the stamina of the car and the skill of the driver."

Al Miller had whipped the Hudson around the 99 curves of that spectacular ascent in 13 minutes, 23-3/5 seconds, cutting 13 seconds from the previous record — set just a year earlier by Chet Miller (no relation), driving, as the press release put it, "another Hudson-built car." And there, in a sense, was the rub: That other "Hudson-built car" had been a Terraplane, of course. For 18 years, ever since the introduction of the first "Super Six," Hudson had care-

by Alex Meredith
photos by Bud Juneau

fully — and successfully — cultivated its reputation as a high-performance automobile. But for the past two seasons it had been totally upstaged by its own "companion" car, the Terraplane.

This time the laurels were claimed in Hudson's own name, and a good thing, too. For in 1933 the Hudson had suffered by far the worst year in its history, with production totaling just 2,401 cars. True, a complete rout had been avoided, thanks to the Terraplane, sales of which outnumbered those of the Hudson by a ratio of nearly 16 to one. But overall, the company's output had fallen slightly from 1932's miserable record — and this at a time when production by the automobile industry as a whole had risen by some 40 percent. Hudson had suffered huge financial losses that year, cutting the company's cash reserves by

one-third. The situation could only be described as desperate!

For three years, 1930-32 inclusive, only eight-cylinder cars had been offered under the Hudson name. "Straight-eights" were in vogue at that time, and for a while the Hudson had been the largest-selling eight in the world. Much less powerful than the F-head Super Six that had preceded it, the Hudson engine of the early thirties was simply an eight-cylinder version of the 1929 Essex "Challenger" power-plant. That it continued to provide the Hudson with creditable performance was due primarily to the fact that the weight of the car had been reduced by some 600 pounds, compared to the 1929 model.

Meanwhile, in 1932 the lower-priced Essex had metamorphosed into the Essex-Terraplane. By stuffing the 70-horsepower Essex engine into a very light, short-wheelbase chassis, Hudson had created a high-stepping automobile whose power-to-weight ratio was said to be the highest in the industry. Intro-

 Originally published in Special Interest Autos #106, Jul.-Aug. 1988

Driving Impressions

Twenty years ago Wayne Ballerstein, of Isleton, California. purchased his 1934 Hudson from a member of San Francisco's hippie colony. It was in sad shape. Headlamps, minus their lenses, were damaged beyond hope. The grille was dented. One rear fender appeared to be a total loss, though in the end it was restored. The bumpers were bent and rusted. and various trim pieces were missing.

And it wouldn't run.

Wayne, who runs a transmission shop in nearby Concord, towed the Hudson to his place of business and tore it apart. The problems with the engine were legion. He found burned valves. bad timing gears, scored bearings — the full catastrophe. In addition to completely rebuilding the straight-eight, Wayne went through the clutch, transmission, differential and brakes, and replaced the seals throughout the chassis.

Then the cosmetic restoration was undertaken. A previous owner had replaced the mohair upholstery. Wayne did the necessary body work, and new paint — in two-tone Sun Tan and Desert Tan, authentic 1934 Hudson colors — was applied by a 72-year-old man who, when this car was built, had been a painter at the Hudson factory. All this was relatively simple. The worst of his problems, Wayne reports, had to do with locating a new pair of headlamps and a whole string of missing trim items. The stylized bird that serves as the radiator ornament was badly bent when it turned up at a swap meet, requiring a very delicate, chancy straightening job. And the hardest piece of all to find was the crank hole cover.

Ballerstein has other Hudsons. His 1939 "112" coupe was the subject of a driveReport in SIA #83, and his '54 Hornet convertible was freshly (and beautifully) restored when Wayne's home community of Isleton, in the San Joaquin River delta was flooded a couple of years ago. Wayne's gorgeous red ragtop was under water up to the tops of the doors. So it sits now in his shop, awaiting a second restoration. He'll freshen up the '34. too, he says. after he retires, in another year or so.

The 1934 coupe, our driveReport car, is the special favorite of Wayne's wife Mary. Two or three times a week she drives it from their riverfront home into the picturesque little village of Isleton. And the Ballersteins have made a number of trips in this car, covering well over 20,000 miles since the mechanical restoration was completed. The usual cruising speed is 55 to 60 miles an hour. Wayne reports, though he has taken it as high as 75 — with plenty of power in reserve.

Like most Hudsons, this one is a brisk performer. In July 1934 the San Francisco Hudson dealer conducted a test in which the car accelerated from rest to 50 mph in just 10 seconds — a phenomenal record by the standards of the time. The test car was fitted with a special 7.00:1 high-compression cylinder head, which obviously gave it an advantage over the stock 5.75:1 version used in Wayne's car. But this one moves out in a hurry, too, and it seems to simply flatten out the hills. On flat terrain it will idle along smoothly in high gear, then pick up speed without downshifting. We haven't found the torque figure for this model, but it must be impressive.

Seating is comfortable in this car, and leg room is ample. The position of the steering wheel, however, is too flat. That is, it's too close to the horizontal for our liking. Almost like the tilt wheel in our lady's Thunderbird when it's in full "up" position, in fact.

We particularly like the Hudson's cork-faced "wet" clutch, the smoothest in the business. It's easier than not, however, to clash the gears when shifting the non-synchro transmission. Steering is comparatively light for a car of this era, and the mechanical brakes are much better than we had anticipated.

For some years we've wanted to road-test a car equipped with the Baker articulated axle (see sidebar, page 26). Now that we have, we don't like it. Wayne's car is susceptible to cross-winds, and it tends to wander a bit, characteristics that are normally quite foreign to a Hudson. Nor does the Axle-Flex (to use Hudson's term for the device) seem to do much for the passengers' comfort. The ride is choppy when the

road is rough, gentle when the pavement is smooth — just about the way it would be with the standard I-beam axle. The front wheels tend to lean sharply in hard cornering, and there have been reports of handling problems when they suddenly snap back to the vertical position — though Wayne tells us he has not encountered that particular difficulty.

Instrumentation is unconventional, but of course Hudson always marched to its own drummer. A water level gauge takes the place of the customary heat indicator. There's an oil level instrument, too, as well as the customary fuel gauge. Problems with the generator and oil pump are indicated by a pair of red warning lights. And this car has the in-dash radio, a comparatively rare accessory in 1934.

There's also an accessory ash tray, affixed to the glove box door. Rather a dumb idea, for when the door is opened the ashes are dumped out onto the floor. Or worse, into the passenger's lap! There are two inside mirrors, for reasons we are unable to fathom. We found them more disconcerting than helpful. The right-hand mirror is fitted with a 30-hour New Haven clock.

When we asked about the absence of windshield wipers — the car is set up for two of them — Mary Ballerstein explained that she was driving along a narrow levee road last winter when three huge tractor-trailer rigs whipped by in close succession. The suction created by their passing simply pulled the wipers loose from their moorings and blew them away. Wayne is looking for replacements, so far without success.

There are some unusual features. The transmission, for instance, locks up and cannot be shifted until the clutch is released. Not a bad idea! And the ventilating wings in the doors can be cranked all the way down if desired. Another good one.

Taken all-in-all, the 1934 Hudson straight-eight is an impressive performer: fast, powerful and sturdy. It's a handsome automobile; and — at $825 for this stylish coupe — it represented a great value for the money, even by Depression standards.

1934 HUDSON

duced with much fanfare in July 1932, the Terraplane promptly began to rack up an impressive series of records in competitive events. The larger (and more expensive) Essex Pacemaker was phased out. And as time went along the hyphenated Essex name was progressively downplayed, until by 1934 the car was known simply as the Terraplane.

For 1933 the Essex Terraplane line was expanded to include an eight-cylinder car, and at mid-year a larger six was added. The eight quickly established an unbeatable reputation for acceleration as well as hill-climbing, and it was advertised as "the roomiest car in the low-priced field."

At the same time, company officials evidently had second thoughts about the elimination of the Hudson Six. In the depression economy of that day, some motorists were hesitant about feeding two extra barrels, and the six-cylinder engine was commencing to experience a resurgence in popularity.

Hudson's response was at once simple and ill-advised. Resurrecting the time-honored Hudson Super Six title, they bestowed it upon a slightly modified version of the 1932 Essex Pacemaker. Smaller, less powerful and much less luxurious than previous Hudsons, it simply didn't live up to the image of the marque. And while it cost $330 less than the cheapest 1932 Hudson, it was still priced $170 higher than the Terraplane Special Six whose wheelbase, engine and other mechanical components it shared. (In fact, the Hudson Super Six actually

1934 Hudson Versus the Competition

	Hudson Dlx 8	Chrysler Six	Graham Deluxe	Hupmobile 417	Nash Big Six	Reo Fl. Cloud	Studebaker Dictator Regal
Price, 2-4 pass. coupe	$855	$755	$855	$795	$785	$845	$775
Shipping weight (lbs.)	2,850	2,903	3,210	2,900	3,340	3,510	3,055
Wheelbase	116″	117″	116″	117″	116″	118″	114″
Cylinders	8	6	6	6	6	6	6
Displacement (cu. in.)	254.47	241.5	224.0	224.0	234.8	268.0	205.3
Horsepower/rpm	108/3,800	93/3,400	85/3,400	80/3,400	88/3,200	85/3,200	88/3,600
Compression ratio	5.75:1	5.4:1	6.5:1	5.32:1	5.25:1	5.3:1	6.3:1
Valve configuration	L-head	L-head	L-head	L-head	OHV	L-head	L-head
Main bearings	5	4	7	4	7	7	4
Indep. front susp?	Optional*	Yes	No	No	Optional*	No	No
Brakes	Mechanical	Hydraulic	Hydraulic	Mechanical	Mechanical	Hydraulic	Mechanical
Braking area (sq. in.)	171.0	177.3	N/a	N/a	166.7	168.0	171.0
Axle ratio	4.11:1	4.11:1	4.27:1	4.36:1	4.44:1	4.30:1	4.55:1
Tire size	6.25/16	6.50/16	6.25/16	6.00/16	5.50/17	6.00/17	5.50/17
HP/c.i.d.	.424	.385	.379	.357	.375	.317	.429
Lbs./HP	26.4	31.2	37.8	36.3	38.0	41.3	34.7
Lbs./c.i.d.	11.2	12.0	14.3	12.9	14.2	13.1	14.9

* Baker Articulated Axle, optional at no additional charge

cost about $80 more than the Terraplane Eight.)

Given the attractive lines, the lively performance, and the outstanding value of the Terraplanes, both six- and eight-cylinder, it would have been difficult to think of a good reason to pay the premium price commanded by the Hudson in 1933. So the severe drop in Hudson sales should have come as no surprise. Clearly, however, it was not a situation that could be tolerated, and for 1934 the product line was completely revamped.

To begin with, the entire line was restyled, with the same body shell serving for both Hudson and Terraplane. The two marques were distinguishable by their different grilles, the Hudson employing a mesh type while the Terraplane used a series of vanes radiating from bottom-center. At the same time the Terraplane's engine compartment was ventilated by means of seven slanted louvers, while the Hudson employed two rows of horizontal doors. Increased length and sweeping new lines made the 1934 models appear lower than before, though in fact they stood an inch and a half taller than the 1933 cars.

The small, 106-inch-wheelbase Terraplane, whose popularity had been overshadowed by that of the larger Special series, was dropped. There were still two distinct Terraplanes, however. The 1934 Standard series, priced with the Chevrolet Master, used a 112-inch chassis, while the Deluxe cars — competing in the Dodge class — were four inches longer.

Powering the 1934 Terraplane was a six-cylinder engine of greater size and power than before. An increase in both bore and stroke gave it a displacement of 212 cubic inches; and 24 was rated at 80 in the Standard series, 85 in the Deluxe — up from 70 the year before.

Just as there were two sizes of Terraplane, so also were there Hudsons of two distinct dimensions. And once again — for the 1934 season only — all Hudsons were eights. Most body styles were fitted to the same 116-inch wheelbase as the senior Terraplanes, but several upscale sedans were offered on a generously

Facing page: driveReport Hudson is brimming with nifty features like roll-down rear window for rumble seat communication/ventilation, and the graceful flying bird radiator mascot. **This page, above:** Even the rumble steps are highly styled. **Left:** But the steel artillery wheels aren't. **Below left and below:** Clever two-way vent window swings in or out or can disappear altogether.

Genealogy of the Hudson Straight-Eight Engine: 1929-1934

YEAR	CAR	CYLINDERS	BORE & STROKE	DISPLACEMENT	HP/RPM
1929	Essex Challenger	6	2.75 x 4.5	160.0	55/3,600
1930	Hudson Great Eight	8	2.75 x 4.5	213.6	80/3,600
1931	Greater Hudson Eight	8	2.875 x 4.5	233.7	87/3,600
1932	Greater Hudson Eight	8	3 X 4.5	254.4	101/3,600
1933	Terraplane Eight	8	2.9375 x 4.5	244.0	94/3,200
1934	Hudson Eight	8	3 x 4.5	254.4	108/3,800

Note: The 1933 Terraplane Eight engine differed in some significant respects from the Hudson Eight of the same year. In addition to its smaller bore (2.9375 inches instead of 3 inches) it featured downdraft carburetion and timing gears in lieu of the Hudson's updraft pot and timing chain. The Hudson Eight of 1934 and later years, while it used the three-inch bore of the 1932-33 Hudson engine, was actually derived from the 1933 Terraplane powerplant and included the latter's carburetion and timing arrangement.

This page: There's no lack of engine ventilation. **Facing page, top and below:** Nor is there a lack of ventilation for driver and passenger. Attractive, sturdy clamp holds windshield in place when open. **Center left:** Access for filling spare is through this handy little door on the tire cover. **Center right:** Sidelamps are miniature versions of headlamps. **Bottom:** Doors have enough handles and grips for two other cars.

The Baker "Articulated Axle"

From time to time throughout the history of the automobile, dramatic new developments have swept the entire industry. Introduced by one manufacturer, they proved to be so popular that the competition scrambled to follow suit. Four-wheel brakes are a case in point. Balloon tires. Downdraft carburetion. The steering-column gearshift. Even free-wheeling, though that one turned out to be a short-lived fad.

There is in the natural order of things something called "The Law of Unintended Consequences," and sometimes, in solving one problem for the motorist, these innovations left another in its place. Take, for instance, four-wheel brakes and balloon tires. Both of these features burst upon the scene in the early twenties, and by 1925 were virtually *de rigueur* for all but the cheapest American cars. The first, of course, made an enormous contribution to the motorist's safety, while the latter was a great benefit to his comfort. But both of these improvements added substantially to the vehicle's unsprung weight, and that's where the mischief started.

Athel F. Denham, writing in *Automotive Industries*, spoke of "the perplexing problems of wheel fight, shimmy, shake, and tramp, which have confronted the industry almost continuously since the introduction of the balloon tire." And of course the front wheel brakes exacerbated the problem by putting a severe horizontal load on springs that were intended to function primarily on a vertical axis.

A number of remedies were tried, with varying degrees of success. Frames were beefed up; "kick-shackles" were fitted; a degree of flexibility was incorporated into the steering linkage. Still the problem remained, and it appeared that the ultimate solution would be found in a concept which had intrigued European engineers for a number of years: independent front suspension.

Hitting the industry full-force in 1934, i.f.s. proved to be one of the most popular innovations of them all. General Motors adopted it throughout the entire line that year, excepting only the little Chevrolet Standard series. In fact, GM went for two distinct types of independent suspension. The system used by Cadillac, Buick and Oldsmobile employed two unequal-length A-brackets, pivoting from the frame, with a vertical coil spring mounted on the lower

bracket. Chevrolet and Pontiac, on the other hand, used the Dubonnet system, a sealed hydraulic unit.

Chrysler, meanwhile, came up with its own version of the double-A-bracket arrangement. So, a year later, did Packard. Studebaker cleverly employed a transverse leaf spring in place of the coils used by the competition. Introducing the system as a 1935 option, they called it "Planar" suspension, and it remained in production as late as 1949.

Ford, of course, remained aloof, sticking to its I-beam axle and buggy-type springs until the introduction of its 1949 models.

Two of the major independent manufacturers, however, elected to take another route. Both Hudson and Nash adopted, as optional equipment on their 1934 models, the "Articulated Axle," manufactured by the Baker Axle Company. A semi- rather than a fully independent suspension system, the Baker arrangement consisted of a conventional I-beam axle in which the center section, between the spring pads, was replaced by a pair of parallel links, one above the other, with cageless roller bearings in the joints. Vertical displacement of either front wheel was permitted by the parallelogram action of the links.

The Baker Articulated Axle, called by Hudson the "Axle-Flex," retained both the semi-elliptic springs and the conventional steering layout, making it inexpensive and readily adaptable to the existing chassis. It was claimed by its manufacturer to break

up front axle harmonics, thus tending to eliminate problems of shimmy and wheel tramp. However, it tended to increase rather than decrease the unsprung weight.

Some engineers hailed the Baker Articulated Axle, at the time of its introduction, as safer and sturdier than the fully independent suspension systems. But in practice it left a good deal to be desired in terms both of performance and durability. Since it was not a fully independent system it managed only a partial solution to the shimmy and related problems, and it failed to achieve the smooth ride that characterized the General Motors and Chrysler suspensions. At the same time, the Articulated Axle created a lot of torque on the front springs, frequently resulting in broken leaves.

Prominently featured among the options available for the 1934 Nash and its companion car, the LaFayette, the Baker axle was conspicuously absent from that company's 1935 sales literature. The 1935 Hudson and Terraplane catalogs continued to offer the "Axle-Flex" option, but the indications are that few cars were so-equipped.

Just as the Baker Articulated Axle was readily adapted to a car with conventional suspension, so also was it easy to convert an Axle-Flex-equipped car to a straight front axle. And evidently that's the fate that has befallen most of them, for it is very seldom nowadays that one encounters a car like our driveReport Hudson — one that is still equipped with the Baker Articulated Axle.

1934 HUDSON

proportioned 123-inch chassis. Prices were as much as $250 lower than the corresponding 1933 models, and only $50 higher than the unpopular Super Six of that ill-fated season.

Powering the 1934 Hudson was a bored-out version of the 1933 Terraplane Eight engine. Its 3-inch by 4.5-inch dimensions were the same as those of the 1933 Hudson Eight, but it incorporated the downdraft carburetor and the timing gears that had been introduced the previous year on the hot-performing Terraplane. It was this engine, periodically updated, that was used in Hudson's eight-cylinder cars right up to the end of the company's straight-eight production in 1952, incidentally. (Similarly, the 3-inch by 5-inch measurements of the 1934 Terraplane powerplant were employed by six-cylinder Hudsons as late as 1947.)

Rated at 108 horsepower in standard form (113 in the long-wheelbase models), the Hudson engine could be purchased with a "Super Power-Dome" high-compression cylinder head which raised its output to 121 horsepower. Since the car was remarkably light — only 2,720 pounds for the bargain-priced Challenger coupe — the power-to-weight ratio was even better than that of the previous year's Terraplane Eight, and of course it was much more favorable than that of the 1934 Terraplane. No longer would the Hudson play second-fiddle to its lower-priced companion car.

New features abounded:

• Draft-free ventilation was provided by means of pivoting vent panes in the front-door windows. Unlike the Fisher "No-Draft" system employed by the contemporary General Motors cars, the Hudson's vent panes could be lowered completely into the doors, if desired.

• In the sedans and coaches the spare tire was concealed behind a flush-fitting door — an industry "first" shared only with Cadillac/LaSalle in 1934, and a trend setter for the industry. For $25.00 extra the spare wheel could be mounted on the right front fender, leaving the rear compartment available for luggage. Cars so-equipped were referred to as "compartment sedans" (four door) and "compartment victorias" (two door).

• A built-in radio was supplied as standard equipment on the Deluxe models, and all closed cars were wired for radio.

• An adjustable steering column was designed to accommodate drivers of every size and shape.

• The starter was activated by means

illustrations by Russell von Sauers, The Graphic Automobile Studio

© copyright 1988, Special Interest Autos

specifications

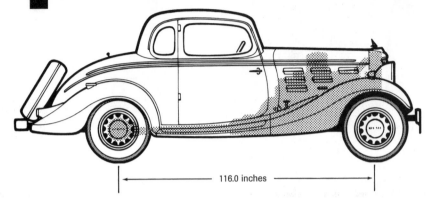
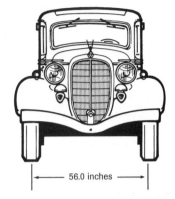

116.0 inches

56.0 inches

1934 Hudson Deluxe Eight

Price	$825 f.o.b. factory, with standard equipment
Standard equipment	Radio, extra quality mohair upholstery, fender lamps, twin horns, dual windshield wipers, twin chromed taillamps, cigar lighter, special door moldings, chromium-plated hood locks

ENGINE

Type	Eight-in-line
Bore/stroke	3 inches x 4½ inches
Displacement	254.47 cubic inches
Max bhp @ rpm	108 @ 3,800
Max torque @ rpm	N/a
Taxable HP	28.8
Compression ratio	5.75:1
Valves	L-head
Main bearings	5
Induction system	Carter W1 1¼-inch downdraft carburetor, camshaft pump
Lubrication system	Splash
Exhaust system	Single
Electrical system	6-volt

CLUTCH

Type	Single wet plate, cork inserts
Diameter	10 inches
Actuation	Mechanical, foot pedal

TRANSMISSION

Type	3-speed selective, floor-mounted lever
Diameter	10 inches
Actuation	Mechanical, foot pedal

TRANSMISSION

Type	3-speed selective, floor-mounted lever
Ratios: 1st	2.42:1
2nd	1.61:1
3rd	1.00:1
Reverse	2.99:1

DIFFERENTIAL

Type	Spiral bevel
Ratio	4.11:1
Drive axles	Semi-floating

STEERING

Type	Gemmer worm-and-sector
Turns, lock to lock	2¾
Ratio	15:1
Turn circle	39 feet, 4 inches

BRAKES

Type	Bendix mechanical, self-energizing
Drum diameter	9 inches
Total swept area	171.0 square inches

CHASSIS & BODY

Frame	Rigid box girder type, 7 inches deep, with X crossmember at center and K-member at front end
Body construction	All steel
Body style	Coupe, 2-4 passenger (with rumble seat)

SUSPENSION

Front	Baker articulated axle, 31-inch longitudinal semi-elliptical springs
Rear	Solid axle, 48¾-inch longitudinal semi-elliptical springs
Tires	6.25/16
Wheels	Steel artillery type

WEIGHTS AND MEASURES

Wheelbase	116 inches
Overall length	194 inches
Overall height	69 inches
Overall width	68 inches
Front track	56 inches
Rear track	56 inches
Ground clearance	8⅛ inches (minimum)
Shipping weight	2,885 pounds

CAPACITIES

Crankcase	7 quarts
Cooling system	23 quarts
Fuel tank	15½ gallons

PERFORMANCE

Top speed (av)	84.91 mph
Acceleration: 0-50	10.8 seconds
0-60	17.0 seconds
Braking distance	33 feet (from 30 mph)

From a road test conducted by *The Autocar*.

CALCULATED DATA

HP/c.i.d.	.424
Pounds/HP	26.7
Pounds/c.i.d.	11.3
Pounds/sq. in. (brakes)	16.9

1934 HUDSON

of a dashboard-mounted solenoid. This, in combination with the new automatic choke, added to the driver's convenience.

• Semi-independent front suspension was provided as a no-cost option in the form of the Baker Articulated Axle. (See sidebar, page 26.)

• Automatic "load-leveler" shock absorbers contributed to a more comfortable ride.

• A water-level indicator on the instrument panel took the place of the customary heat indicator. (Having adopted thermostatic heat control for 1934, Hudson evidently deemed the temperature gauge to be unnecessary.)

• A new cam follower permitted the valves a much longer dwell at wide-open position and more rapid opening and closing, contributing to the engine's increased power.

Hudson's engineering practices were always somewhat unconventional, and

the 1934 models continued a number of the company's time-honored traditions:

• Engine blocks were cast of high chrome alloy steel, making them among the hardest in the industry.

• Internal lubrication was by the splash system, rather than the usual pressure pump.

• Pistons were made of low expansion silicon-aluminum alloy in lieu of the cast iron that was then in general use.

• Piston rings were pinned in place. (Hudson liked to boast that only one other manufacturer In the world fol-

Left: Dash has attractive woodgrain finish. *Below left:* 254-cubic-inch flathead straight eight powers the Hudson. *Below:* Hudson was one of the first to use "idiot lights" instead of analog oil and amp gauges. *Bottom:* Even from the back, where the styling of many thirties cars falls down, the Hudson presents a sleek, pleasing appearance.

lowed that practice: Rolls-Royce.)

• A wet clutch was used. Oil-cushioned, it featured a cork-inserted clutch plate for smooth, easy engagement. (An automatic clutch was optionally available.)

And of course, in the Hudson tradition the car carried fewer pounds per horsepower than any other automobile in its price class: 26.4 in the case of the four-passenger coupe, compared to 31.2 pounds for the equivalent Chrysler, 38 pounds for the Nash. Similarly, the Hudson engine developed more power in relation to its displacement than any of its competitors with the exception of Studebaker's new Dictator Six.

Not surprisingly, given the attractive lines of its new cars and the superb values they represented, the Hudson Motor Car Company scored a rousing comeback in 1934. Overall, production for the calendar year more than doubled, while sales of cars bearing the Hudson name rose ten times over.

It was one thing to build more cars; it proved to be quite another to turn a profit. Once again in 1934, Hudson's ledgers were written in red. A substantial price hike in April evidently had a dampening effect upon sales, and a partial rollback took place two months later. Seemingly, Hudson was offering too much car for the dollar, and there wasn't any profit in it, yet the competitive situation was such that the company dared not raise its prices very much. Not until the following year, 1935, would the Hudson Motor Car Company be restored to profitability.

The proliferation of series and models

was astounding. Hudson and Terraplane each offered three distinct trim levels and an amazing array of body styles. So much variety could not possibly have been good business practice, for — including limited-production types such as the Hudson roadster — there were at least 25 Hudsons and 18 Terraplanes to choose from. Pity the poor dealer, who couldn't possibly afford to stock them all! ☙

Acknowledgments and Bibliography

The Autocar, *July 13, 1934;* Automobile Trade Journal, *January and April 1934;* Automotive Industries, *various issues;* Don Butler, History of Hudson; John Conde, The Cars that Hudson Built; Hudson factory literature; Hudson-Essex-Terraplane Club literature; Beverly Rae Kimes and Henry Austin Clark, Jr. (editors), Standard Catalog of American Cars, 1805-1942.

Our thanks to John Bond, Escondido, California; Ray Borges, William F. Harrah Automobile Foundation, Reno, Nevada; Dave Brown, Durham, California; Tom and Lynn Burke, Concord, California; Mandy Eastus, Isleton, California; Wayne and Chris Graefen, Fullerton, California; Press and Janet Kale, Buena Park, California; Evelyn Silva, Isleton, California. Special thanks to Wayne and Mary Ballerstein, Isleton, California.

1936

HUDSON RARELY did anything by the book and almost always added those extra little somethings that caught you off guard. Like twin decklid handles when you had an armful of groceries. Or tiny double cover doors on the rear-seat ashtray. Twin gloveboxes, one being the access panel to get behind the dashboard. An early flow-through ventilation system that actually worked, odd as it was. Optional pre-selector gearshift and vacuum clutch that, with the proper voodoo, almost amounted to an automatic transmission.

Some of the Hudson oddments became traditional: Oil-cushioned clutch with bottle-stopper facings. A mechanical reserve braking system below the regular hydraulic system, so if a brake line burst, you could still slide the rear tires. Idiot lights the size of ruby shooters. An emergency brake handle whose casting and location the company used until it merged with Nash. And a 3-main-bearing 6 that on paper looked like it couldn't last a week but in fact was one of the most willing, durable, and longest-lived flatheads ever built (although rife with compromises).

Our 1936 driveReport Terraplane now belongs to Robert (Andy) Dunlap of Reno, Nevada. Andy had no intention of buying anything like this car until he saw it. The original owner was a little old lady in Washington State, who put all of about 50,000 miles on it, driving it only in dry weather and always keeping it garaged. The car stood in dead storage for at least 20 years.

In late 1970, she gave it to her grandson, who drove it to the University of Washington for a few months and then decided to sell it. To do this, he made a quick trip in it to Reno and knocked on the door of Harrah's Automobile Collection, hoping they'd buy it. When Harrah's didn't, the grandson got a little desperate for cash and contacted the local chapter of the Hudson-Essex-Terraplane Club. Andy, who is past president of the Northern Nevada chapter, heard about the car's condition, and he merely wanted to look at

it, but when he saw it (and it *is* mint), he headed right for the bank. Andy, who's a partner in the CPA firm of Elmer Fox & Co., has owned the car since July 1971. The odometer showed 52,000 miles when we drove it.

This Terraplane is a car that loves to be lugged. You can crawl up to a red light at no more than 3-4 mph, then on green merely bear down easy on the accelerator and, without buck, balk, snatch, or strain, the car moves right out. Performance is fairly brisk through the gears, and Reid Railton, driving basically this same car in 1935, did 0-50 mph in 14.05 seconds under AAA sanction at Bonneville. That's about a second slower than a 1936 Ford.

Unlike the Ford, the Terraplane 6 runs out of revs pretty early. The 4.11 rear-axle ratio contributes. Speeds over 50 mph begin to leave the 212-inch 6 winded, and at 50 we felt too sorry for the splasher to keep pushing. The factory offered an optional 2-barrel carb and an aluminum head that gave 100 bhp instead of Andy's 88. These might have helped, but what this car really needs is overdrive, and Hudson didn't offer that until 1940.

Andy Dunlap's Terraplane does have Electric Hand, but unfortunately it was disconnected, so we used the floor lever. In shifting the non-synchro gearbox, we found that any hesitation on our parts made for crunch. Quick, jabbing shifts slide in easy as pie. Hudson included a gear interlock system this year that holds the transmission in gear until you de-clutch. In other words, you can't shift until you shove in the clutch pedal. (By the way, you also can't start the engine until you do the same, although the starter button is on the dashboard, not beneath the pedal.)

Steering feels heavy at low speeds but lightens up as the car gets rolling. It's much quicker than most, with only 3-3/4 turns lock to lock.

Brakes are excellent—very light, almost touchy, yet precise and positive. 1936 was the first year for Hudson's Duo-Automatic brake arrangement—the mechanical reserve system

Did Ford say its 1973 mini-vents are new? Terraplane's front quarter panes crank up out of door, then can be turned to direct blast of air.

All four doors hinge from rear, which eases entry and exit but spells danger if they're opened accidentally while the Terraplane is at speed.

Originally published in Special Interest Autos #12, Aug.-Sept. 1972

Terraplane

driveReport

by Bill Williams, *Associate Editor*

Instrument cluster drapes over top of dash, with the twin gloveboxes at either side and Bendix Electric Hand unit at column. Previous owner disconnected preselector, snapped in floor lever.

mentioned previously. We've never had an opportunity to test those bottom two inches of pedal, but we've heard from people who have used them that in a pinch they're better than a sharp stick.

The Terraplane's flow-through ventilation system makes another interesting conversation piece. There's this 8 x 10-inch hole underneath the rear seat cushion, just above the differential housing. Covering the hole is a cloth screen inside a wire-loaded leather collar. Air can pass upward through this hole as you drive along—it is drawn into the passenger area by vacuum created by the venturi action of cracking open the front vent panes. So air comes up from under the back seat and distributes itself around the car interior, then passes out the front quarter panes.

We tried this system on a hot Reno day, and yes, it does work, though like most flow-throughs, it's not perfect. On dirt roads, a little dust draws up through the hole when it's kicked up by the front tires. And as in GM's flow-through system of 1970-71, that hole in the rear puts a blast of cold wind on rear passengers' wallets in wintertime.

The Terraplane's instruments, draped as they are over the top center of the dashboard (we call them Dali dials, because they're bent like Dali's famous molten watches), are by no means easy to see. They stand at about 45° to the driver's normal line of sight, so he's looking off across the road every time he glances at the gauges. About the only advantage to this system is that it was easy to convert the car to right-hand drive, and since Hudson did a fair amount of exporting to England in those days, it wasn't an altogether thoughtless arrangement (nor were the double gloveboxes, for the same reason).

In the summer of 1932, when the first Essex Terraplane debuted, it stood on a 106-inch wheelbase, same as Ford's, and sold for a base price of $425, which was actually lower than either Ford or Chevrolet. But by 1936, the Terraplane's wheelbase had grown nine inches and its price was about $100 more, model for model, than Ford and Chevy. The Terraplane's resale value wasn't quite so good as the Big Three's. A quick check into the Kelley Blue Book for Jul.-Aug. 1939 shows that a 1936 Terraplane, which cost $720 new, was worth $250 three years later. A comparable 1936 Ford sedan brought $265 at that time, and a 1936 Chevrolet 4-door commanded $300 on used car lots.

Brochures call it a 6-passenger sedan, but we'd rate it more like five. We found it comfortable both front and rear, with tremendous back-seat leg room, and head room like a cathedral. We can imagine the argument that must have gone on over that ceiling. Frank Spring, Hudson's chief stylist, liked low cars, but most of the management people insisted on a car tall enough for a man to wear a hat in. Roads being bumpy in those days, there also had to be jounce room between the man's hat and the roof. So, guess who won.

Roy Chapin had been away from Hudson for 1-1/2 years during the Depression to serve as Hoover's Secretary of Commerce. What a time to be Secretary of Commerce! He returned to Hudson in 1933 and then died suddenly of a heart attack in February 1936.

Everyone knew ahead of time that when Chapin left Hudson's presidency, A.E. Barit would take over. Barit had been Chapin's right hand, but he was a completely different sort of man. Whereas Chapin ran the company from inside the plant, Barit ran it from behind a desk. He'd come up through the accounting and pur-

Hudson-Bendix Electric Hand

The 1935 Hudson and Terraplane became the first U.S. cars to adopt Bendix's new preselector shift control, Electric Hand. Briefly, here's how it works.

There's a tiny H-pattern shift gate that stands on a short stalk just below the steering wheel rim. The driver can select a gear with the fingertips of his right hand. The act of depressing the clutch then shifts the gears. Hudson also offered an optional Bendix vacuum clutch, and with both extras, the driver shifted by merely lifting his foot off the gas pedal.

He could preselect any gear at any time, and the shift wouldn't occur until he worked either the clutch or accelerator. With Electric Hand in use, the normal floor-mounted gear-shift lever was removed and stored in the right-hand kick panel, but any time he wanted to, the driver could lock out the preselector with an on-off switch on the stalk, plug in the floor lever (it snapped in easily), and shift gears manually.

Mechanically, Electric Hand is fairly simple. It has two vacuum cylinders mounted onto the transmission. One cylinder controls the back-and-forth movement of the conventional H shift pattern (through neutral), and the other controls ahead-and-back (low, 2nd, 3rd, and reverse gears). Signals to the vacuum cylinders come via electric switches inside the fingertip unit, passed along through relays and solenoids. The only difference in construction of the transmission is a new cover design for the shift mechanism. Hudson also chamfered the gears differently to make shifts quieter and, although the gearbox wasn't synchromesh, it did use dog clutches to aid shifting.

Electric Hand remained a factory-installed option from 1935 through 1938. It cost $20 in 1935 and $22.50 for 1937. Cord had the same basic preselector in 1936-37, and it made a lot more sense for this fwd car. Owners of Electric Hand soon found that the unit gave a fair amount of trouble. It tended to short and needed constant minor attention and adjustment. Most owners eventually disconnected it.

The Bendix preselector was by no means this country's first or only. Other versions had been around for at least 15 years, perhaps longer. Development of the Bendix unit was done in its B-K (Bragg-Kliesrath) Div., which started life by manufacturing vacuum brake boosters. Victor Kliesrath (see 1934 SWC Bendix driveReport, *SIA* #8, pp.40-45) brainstormed both the Bendix vacuum clutch, introduced on 1932 Hudsons, and Electric Hand.

About a year after the Bendix preselector came on the market, another very similar unit did, too—the Evans Auto-Shift. This was developed by E.G. Hill and H.W. Hey of Automatic Shifters Co., then bought out by Evans. The Evans Auto-Shift was simpler than the Bendix unit, but so far as we know, it was never offered optionally by any automaker. Evans did supply vacuum shifters (non-preselect) and clutches to various manufacturers, among them Graham, Nash, and Studebaker.

One final postscript: Hudson was safety conscious, and Electric Hand was touted not only as a convenience but also as a safety feature. It left the driver's hands on the wheel at all times. Other Hudson safety items for 1936 were its Duo-Automatic reserve braking system, one-piece all steel top, no-dip front axle design, optional directional signals, and optional "safety swinging" brake lamp that rocked back and forth whenever the brakes were applied.

chasing ranks, and Barit was much more a pencil pusher than a car man.

He'd come into the company along with Chapin in 1909, then aged 20, starting out as a secretary to the purchasing agent. He then moved up, and all his positions kept him close to Hudson's suppliers. He later became company treasurer, then general manager, and finally president, a position he held until Hudson merged with Nash in '54, (Roy D. Chapin Jr., who's now board chairman of American Motors, is the elder Chapin's son.)

Barit ran a fairly conservative ship, not made less so when Stuart Baits became Hudson's general manager, vice president, and a member of the board in 1936. Baits had been Hudson's chief engineer for years, and he had what amounted to a mania for splasher engines.

It wouldn't hurt to turn back a moment and talk about the Terraplane's 6-cylinder engine, because that history sheds light not only on Hudson but also on Baits.

Here's a flathead 6 that saw production for 24 long years—1924 through 1947. It started out as an absolutely terrible engine for the first Essex 6 of 1924. What made it so awful was an inadequate oil supply (dippers and oil feed to the front main only) and only three mains. Now three mains weren't so bad in themselves, because Marmon, Pontiac, Chevrolet, and later Hudson 6s used only three for years and got along just fine. But as the oil got hot in this Essex 6, very little of it reached the center main nor #6 rod bearing, and one or the other would usually melt. A wild 5.60:1 rear axle didn't exactly help.

Hudson replaced plenty of Essex engines free when they burned up under warranty. Later, when Hudson charged a $50 replacement fee, they still got lots of takers. As John Bond pointed out in "A Field Day of Fiascos" (*SIA* #7. pp 16-19), that initial Essex 6 was one of the industry's all-time great mistakes.

Hudson clung to it doggedly, though, and Baits did a slow but remarkable job of improving it. The basic problem before 1927 was an inadequate plunger-type oil pump. In 1930, Hudson

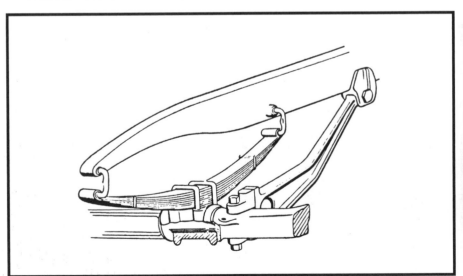

The 1936 Terraplane's solid front axle uses radius rods that help to locate it; thus the car can have more flexible springs. The rods also prevent nosedive on hard braking and act as stabilizer bars.

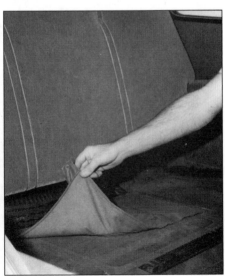

Air for Terraplane's flow-through vent system enters here, gets filtered by cloth beneath seat.

Tall trunk takes judicious packing, with spare, tools occupying most of lower compartment.

This is the Custom 4-door sedan, as distinguished by flat decklid. Touring sedan had ballooned-out trunk, and lids interchanged. Twin handles present challenge as they must be turned together.

AMERICAN MOTORS CORP., JOHN CONDE

One-piece plastic panel has thin sections that light at night; idiot lamps for oil, generator.

Optional defogger duct popped from right-hand "glovebox." Door also gave access behind dash.

brought out the Greater 8, which was merely the Essex 6 with two more cylinders. But the 8 couldn't get by with oil feed to the front of the pan only, so Baits developed a double-acting pump that fed oil to the front and the rear at the same time. Again, though, the 8 stuck with dippers. Baits, in fact, refused to go to full pressure until the re-engineered Hudson 6 of 1948.

At any rate, when the 8 got oil feed to both ends in 1930, so did the Essex 6 (same pump). In 1934, when the 6 got its final reaming to 3 x 5 inches (212 cid), Baits tossed in a redesigned pump that gave twice the flow, and that finally brought the engine up to date.

The three mains did grow a little in later years, and almost every other component was re-engineered in that decade 1924-34, including eliminating roller tappets, going to 4-ring pistons, bigger valve stems and springs, etc., etc., etc., etc.

With all due respect to the 3 x 5 Terraplane and Hudson 6 of 1934-47, it was durable and reliable but filled with compromises. Cylinders were siamesed in threes, with only 5/32 inch of metal between the barrels. Bore distortion was horrible with temperature changes, and for this reason the Terraplane went to pinned rings in 1934. Normal rings wouldn't seat as they moved around in out-of-round cylinders. Yet Hudson made public a series of dyno tests conducted on the 212 engine in Nov. 1934. Here, after running at full throttle for 208 hours, simulating speeds of 71-89 mph, the engine averaged 322 miles per quart of oil (no great shakes); teardown showed *no ring wear, no*

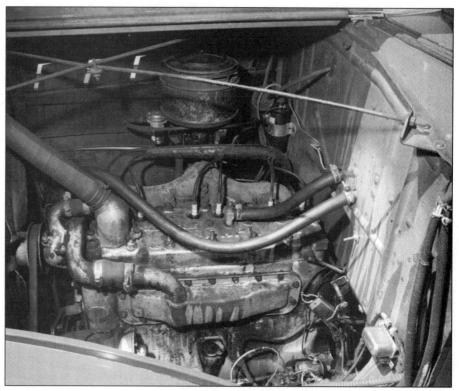

Venerable 3 x 5 Hudson 6 cranks out 88 bhp. Andy Dunlap degreased engine just before we took photos, *but didn't have a chance to repaint it. This same 3-main engine was used through 1947.*

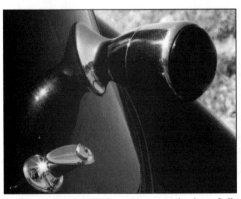

A small handle above rear quarter window rolls glass back about 3 inches. By cracking the front vents and these rear panes, air circulates gently throughout Terraplane's passenger compartment.

Twin rear ashtray doors aren't better than one, but we admire Hudson's attention to detail.

Flying plastic carrot could be wired to light up, helps driver "aim" car in lane — day or night.

By unclipping this portion of center grille bar, crank could be inserted for dead-battery starts.

AMERICAN MOTORS CORP., JOHN CONDE

Big potmetal taillight castings weigh about 3 lb. each, make raising decklid harder than most.

Hudson president A.E. Barit (left) and chief engineer Stuart Baits ponder a blueprint in 1936.

1936 Terraplane

piston wear, minimal bore taper, some checking of #2 and #4 con rod bearings, and the engine needed a valve job to bring back maximum power. Not bad all in all, and an admirably honest review of performance by the factory.

Still, too many people remembered the Essex's reputation. Funny thing about Essex. In 1929, it pushed the company into the #3 spot in national new-car sales. Now that's quite a feat when you think about it—an independent like Hudson hitting third.

Yet by 1930, the year the company made an acceptable engine out of the 1924 fiasco, Essex's reputation finally caught up with it and people switched to other sixes, notably Pontiac and Chevrolet.

Hudson went through five straight years of red ink during the Depression, losing a total of more than $15 million between 1931 and 1935. Blackest year was 1932, coinciding with the Essex Terraplane's intro.

It's beyond the scope of this driveReport to go into the interesting Essex Terraplane period. We'll leave that for another time. Suffice it to say that the Essex Terraplane 6 of 1932-33 and the Essex Terraplane 8 of 1933 still rank with the hillclimb greats of all time. It was the Essex Terraplane that gave later Terraplanes their reputation for speed and stamina. Yet the later Terraplane never pulled off anything like those 1932-33 records.

Hudson had always been very aggressive in the area of speed, and in the early 1930s, a Hudson engineer named R.G. (Buddy) Marr created what became a factory performance team. It wasn't Hudson's first, but Marr hired the Miller Brothers, Al and Chet, and together these three campaigned Hudsons and Terra-planes throughout the 1930s, setting hundreds of hillclimb, speed, endurance, and economy records. They covered the country from New Hampshire to California.

Again, the whole story would fill a book, so we'll touch on it just lightly. Buddy Marr's idea was to make Hudson a household word by bringing records to each section of the country locally. In a well-mapped-out, concerted program, he and the Millers drove to practically every section of the country and set hillclimb records everywhere. These were national records set on the local level, so home-town people could watch and read about them with a personal involvement. Marr and the Millers would sometimes run up two and three mountains a day, and they'd drive from town to town in the same cars that set the records.

But it turned out to be just too much work, so Marr moved on to the Indy 500 with a Hudson 8 stock blocker, to Muroc dry lake in California, Bonneville in Utah, and Daytona Beach, setting records at all those places, too. Some of them stood for decades; others were broken again and again by subsequent Hudsons. Marr was also friendly with such speed stars as Malcolm Campbell and Reid Railton, and on several occasions he talked those two into setting records in Hudsons, thereby attaching their names to the factory's in record books.

After 1933, though, Terraplane didn't set many new marks. It did set eight Class C and Unlimited records at Bonneville in 1937, but these were bro-

1936 Hudson Terraplane Custom 6-62
4-door sedan

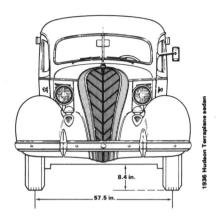

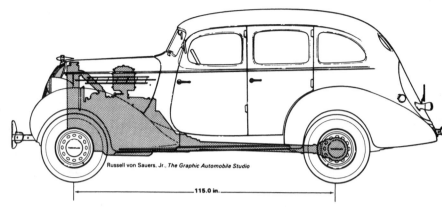

Russell von Sauers. Jr.. *The Graphic Automobile Studio*

1936 Hudson Terraplane sedan

8.4 in.

57.5 in.

115.0 in.

Price when new $720 f.o.b. Detroit (1936).

Current valuation*   Xlnt. $2,100; gd. $870; fair $350.

Options   Electric Hand, glovebox light, bumper guards.

ENGINE
Type   L-head, in-line 6, cast en bloc, water cooled, 3 mains, circulating and splash lubrication.
Bore & stroke   3.00 x 5.00 in.
Displacement   212.1 cid.
Max. bhp @ rpm..   .88 @ 3,800.
Max. torque @ rpm   N.a.
Compression ratio.   6.0:1.
Induction system.   1 -bbl. Carter downdraft carb, mechanical fuel pump.
Exhaust system   Cast-iron manifold, single muffler.
Electrical system   6-volt battery/coil.

CLUTCH
Type   Oil cushioned single wet plate, cork lining.
Diameter   8.625 in.
Actuation   Mechanical, foot pedal.

TRANSMISSION
Type   3-speed manual, preselector (disconnected), floor lever.
Ratios: 1st   2.42:1.
         2nd   1.61:1.
         3rd   1 00:1.
         Reverse   2.99:1.

DIFFERENTIAL
Type   Spiral bevel gears.
Ratio   4.11:1.
Drive axles   Semi-floating.

STEERING
Type   Gemmer worm & sector.
Turns lock to lock   3.75.
Ratio   17:1.
Turn circle   44.0 ft.

BRAKES
Type   4-wheel hydraulic drums with mechanical reserve, internal expanding.
Drum diameter   10.0625 in.
Total lining area   154.0 sq. in.

CHASSIS & BODY
Frame   Channel-section steel, double dropped, central X-member.
Body construction   All steel.
Body style   4-dr., 5-pass. sedan.

SUSPENSION
Front   I-beam axle, longitudinal radius rods & semi-elliptic leaf springs, tubular hydraulic shock absorbers.
Rear   Solid axle, longitudinal leaf springs, tubular hydraulic shock absorbers.
Tires   6.00 x 16 tube type, 4-ply.
Wheels   Pressed steel, drop-center rims, lug-bolted to brake drums.

WEIGHTS & MEASURES
Wheelbase   115.0 in.
Overall length   195.0 in.
Overall height   70.75 in.
Overall width   70.0 in.
Front tread   56.0 in.
Rear tread   57.5 in.
Ground clearance   8.4 in.
Curb weight   2,810 lb.

CAPACITIES
Crankcase   6.0 qt.
Cooling system   13 qt.
Fuel tank   16.5 gal.

FUEL CONSUMPTION
Best   18-20 mpg.
Average   15-17 mpg.

PERFORMANCE (from *The Autocar* test of 1935 Terraplane sedan):
0-50mph   15.4 sec.
0-60 mph   23.0 sec.
0-70 mph   37.4 sec.
Top speed   80.36 mph.

*Courtesy *Antique Automobile Appraisal*, Prof. Barry Hertz.

ken almost immediately by a Hudson 8. Reid Railton drove a 1935 Terraplane to an average of 24.24 mpg at 28 mph, but other than that, Terraplane had to be satisfied with hanging onto Hudson's coattails.

Some people were surprised to see Hudson drop the Essex name after 1933, but there'd been little choice. Essex was simply a car *non grata*. Besides, the vogue was to bring out less expen-

sive companion models with completely different names—Rockne, Viking, Marquette, LaFayette. So Terraplane it became.

The Terraplane was better built than it had any right to be. It was good value for the money if you kept one long enough. As the 1930s ripened, Terraplanes got bigger and more like Hudsons. For 1938, the name was changed to Terraplane Hudson, and the lowest-priced Hudson that year

became the 112. For 1939, the Terraplane name evaporated, its place taken by the Hudson 112.

Special thanks to John Bond, Newport Beach, Calif; Robert Dunlap, Reno, Nev.; John A. Conde of American Motors, Detroit; G.K. Renner, Joplin. Mo.; and a half-dozen sharp-eyed members of the Hudson-Essex-Terra-plane Club, 23104 Dolorosa, Woodland Hills, CA 91364.

1939 HUDSON 112

drive report

HEIR TO THE ESSEX

by Arch Brown
photos by Jim Tanji

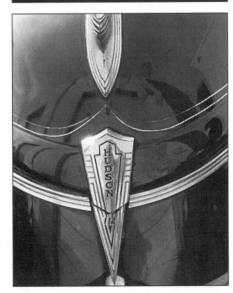

OR years. Hudson had tried to establish a beachhead in the lowest priced field, first with the Essex and then with the Terraplane.

It's not that the Essex started out that way. Its $1,395 price tag at the time of its introduction, back in 1919, had put it solidly in the medium-price range — $600 below the Hudson, to be sure, but $300 higher than the Dodge. Powered by a sturdy, 50-horsepower, F-head 4-banger, the Essex quickly earned an outstanding reputation for both durability and performance. Before the new car had been on the market for a year, it set a world long-distance record by traveling 3,037 miles in 50 hours — a whisker over 60 mph average!

By 1922 the Essex's horsepower had been raised to 55 and the price of the touring car had been cut to $1,095, only $110 more than the Dodge. Even more significantly, the company introduced the coach, a fully enclosed two-door sedan priced at $1,495 — and reduced before the year was out to $1,345. This was at a time when a Model T Ford cen-

ter-door sedan sold for nearly twice the price of a conventional touring car, and an enclosed Buick commanded a $700 premium over the open model. So the Essex coach, in providing closed-car comfort at a minimal price premium, proved to be a trendsetter for the entire industry.

There was more to come. For 1924 Essex introduced its first six (see sidebar, page 38), simultaneously lowering the price of the coach to $975. And the following year that figure was cut to $895, five dollars below the price of the open touring car. As General Motors president Alfred P. Sloan, Jr. was later to relate, "Nothing like that had ever been seen before in the automobile industry, and the Essex coach had considerable vogue."

Indeed, Hudson produced more than a quarter of a million automobiles that year, most of them Essex coaches. That represented a fifteenfold increase over 1919, the year of the Essex's debut. Other manufacturers scrambled to follow suit, and before long the closed car

Originally published in Special Interest Autos #83, Sept.-Oct. 1984

had replaced the touring as the dominant body style.

Of course, pioneering the concept of a reasonably priced enclosed automobile wasn't the same thing as producing a low-priced car. Ford's tudor sedan, while double the price of the Model T touring ($580 versus $290), was still $315 cheaper than the 1924 Essex coach. But cost-cutting efforts continued, and even as Ford's prices were rising, the tab for the Essex was being shaved. By 1929, a banner year in which it turned out more than 300,000 cars, the Hudson Motor Car Company enjoyed — albeit briefly — the distinction of ranking third in the industry. And the price difference between the Essex and Ford's Model A was down to $170.

Then came the Great Depression. Automobile sales plummeted, with independent firms like Hudson taking a far worse beating than their larger rivals. By 1931 Hudson-Essex production had fallen to less than a fifth of the 1929 figure, and Hudson found itself in seventh place, industry-wide. The company lost nearly $2 million that year, and unspecified "unusual expenditures" — product development, possibly — ate away another $6.5 million of Hudson's cash reserves. Clearly, desperate measures were called for!

And so, in July 1932 Hudson mounted its first full-scale assault on the low-priced field. They called the new car the Essex Terraplane, and it combined the 70-horsepower Essex engine with a lightweight, short-wheelbase chassis to provide the most favorable power-to-weight ratio in its field. They priced the new car at $475, $25 below Ford's high-stepping new V-8.

At last, Hudson really had a low-priced car. But the new model had a less-than-standard tread, and its narrow width tended to make it look tall and ungainly. Its comparatively diminutive size also drew a negative reaction from many observers. And so, as time went along the Terraplane (the Essex prefix having been dropped after 1933) began to grow — in size, in power and in price. By 1935 it cost $115 more than the Ford, and only $40 less than the increasingly popular Pontiac.

Prices jumped again in mid-1937, by nearly 29 percent this time. No longer could the Terraplane have any pretensions of being a "low-priced" car. At $805 for the cheapest five-passenger model, it actually cost $30 more than the Chrysler Royal. The public didn't know it, but the stage was being set for a new, smaller Hudson, the one that would return the company to the hotly competitive low-priced field.

The announcement came in January 1938. It had been preceded by a series of "teaser" ads which promised "A *new* lowest-priced car, which will give to its owners a combination of size. room, smooth performance, sturdiness, and safety on the one hand...and remarkably low cost of ownership and operation on the other...such as has never been offered in any other lowest-priced car.

"The car will be offered," the ads went on to declare. "by the one manufacturer who is fully qualified by experience, plant facilities and methods, and organization set-up to produce this really new type of lowest-priced car....

"In short, here will be a better deal for the lowest-price car buyer's dollar...."

An advertising blitz followed the introduction of the new model, known as the Hudson 112. And when the opportunity came for Hudson to provide the pace car for the Indianapolis 500, the company passed over the 122 horsepower Hudson eight — the obvious

The Genealogy of the Hudson 112

The following table gives selected specifications of Hudson's lowest-priced series for each year from 1924 through 1939. Prices shown refer to the least expensive five-passenger closed car produced by Hudson. Ford prices are given for comparative purposes.

Year	Model	Bore x Stroke	Displacement	Horsepower	Wheelbase	Weight	Price	Price, Ford[1]
1924	Essex Six	25.625" x 4"	129.2[2]	29	110.5"	2,305	$975	$590
1925	Essex Six	2.6875" x 4.25"	144.7	37	110.5"	2,370	$895	$580
1926	Essex Six	2.6875" x 4.25"	144.7	40	110.5"	2,455	$765	$495
1927	Essex Six	2.6875" x 4.5"	153.2[3]	44	110.5"	2,450	$735	$495
1928	Essex Challenger	2.625" x 4.5"	147.0	44	110.5"	2,560	$735	$550
1929	Essex Challenger	2.75" x 4.5"	160.4	55	110.5"	2,635	$695	$525
1930	Essex Challenger	2.75" x 4.5"	160.4	58	113"	2,730	$765	$490
1931	Essex Super Six	2.875" x 4.5"	175.3	60	113"	2,690	$595	$490
1932	Essex Terraplane	2.9375" x 4.75"	193.1	70	106"	2,205	$475	$500
1933	Essex Terraplane	2.9375" x 4.75"	193.1	70	106"	2,335	$525	$500
1934	Terraplane	3" x 5"	212.1	80	112"	2,600	$575	$535
1935	Terraplane	3" x 5"	212.1	88	112"	2,610	$625	$510
1936	Terraplane	3" x 5"	212.1	88	115"	2,715	$615	$520
1937	Terraplane	3" x 5"	212.1	96	117"	2,830	$625[4]	$610
1938	Hudson 112	3"x4.125"	174.9	83	112"	2,595	$724	$665
1939	Hudson 112	3"x4.125"	174.9	86	112"	2,682	$775	$680

[1]Ford prices from 1932 on refer to V-8 cars (excluding 60-hp); all prices shown are at introduction.
[2]supplanted by 144.7 c.i.d. engine on 6/23/24.
[3]Second series, introduced 6/25/27. Earlier cars used 144.7 c.i.d. engine
[4]Raised to $805 at mid-year.

The Six That Made a Big Splash

There was nothing really new about the engine that powered the Hudson 112. Essentially, it was an updated version of the old "splasher" first introduced in the 1924 Essex.

A puny little piece of machinery it had been then, displacing only 129.9 cubic inches and developing a scant 29 horsepower. Hudson made much of its six-cylinder smoothness, and in that respect it really did represent a distinct improvement over the F-head four-banger that it replaced. But its horsepower wasn't much more than half that of the old four, and almost literally it wouldn't pull the hat off your head! And to make matters worse, the splash lubrication system didn't work very well, partly because of its totally inadequate 3.5-quart oil capacity and partly due to certain deficiencies in its design.

Essex's hard-won reputation as a fast, tough, dependable car suffered badly at the hands of that first six, and within a few months the initial steps were taken to rectify the situation. Bore and stroke were increased, yielding a badly needed 27.5 percent boost in power, while a redesigned oil pan with greater capacity and improved baffling eliminated some of the engine's tendency to fry its own bearings.

Still, there were complaints. Partly, the problem lay in the engine's principal virtue: its smoothness. For it posed a constant temptation to the driver, to push the little mill — which still displaced only 144.7 cubic inches — beyond any reasonable limits. It simply wasn't designed to be driven flat-out for extended periods, and it wreaked its revenge upon those owners who subjected it to that sort of abuse.

Improvements continued to be made. A longer stroke in mid-1927 was accompanied by greater main bearing surfaces, and by 1930 the crankshaft itself was strengthened as well. Displacement continued to grow, to 160.4 cubic inches in 1929, 175.3 in 1931, 193.1 a year later, and finally to 212.1 in 1934. By that time, of course, the Essex had metamorphosed into the Terraplane, and a high-compression version of the same engine was employed for the six-cylinder Hudson as well.

In fact, from 1930 onward there was an eight-cylinder variation on the Essex theme, used to power the Hudson Greater Eight and its successors. It, too, was too small for the job at first. Displacing only 213.8 cubic inches in its initial form, it was an anemic replacement for the lusty, 288.6-c.i.d. six whose place it took. And again, there was some damage to

the Hudson Motor Car Company's image. But like its six-cylinder counterpart, the eight began to grow — rapidly, in this instance. For 1931 it was bored to 233.7 cubes, corresponding to the increased bore used for the Essex six. And the following year it was bored again, yielding 254.5 cubic inches from a 3-inch by 4.5-inch bore and stroke.

Terraplane, meanwhile, offered a straight eight of its own — for just one year, 1933. This powerplant was a slightly smaller but substantially improved version of the eight-cylinder unit being used for the Hudson, and as recounted by Norm Mason in *SIA* #38, it became the basis for all Hudson eights from 1934 through 1952.

Meanwhile, good things were happening to the Essex-cum-Hudson six. An improved pump, introduced in 1932, provided better distribution of the oil, while redesigned baffles and more adequate dippers did their part to assure proper lubrication. A new crankshaft featuring integral counter-weights was fitted in 1934. The splasher had come into its own, and once again, as in the heyday of the Hudson Super Six, Hudson-built automobiles were racking up records in competitive events all over the country.

And so, when it came time to develop an engine suitable for the 112 series, Hudson had the perfect foundation. For the lighter car a smaller displacement would be appropriate, and of course increased economy was one of the company's major objectives in developing the 112. The solution was simply to shorten the stroke of the Hudson (and Terraplane) engine from 5 inches to 4.125 inches, reducing its displacement from 212.1 to 174.9 cubic inches. At the same time, in the interest of maintaining an acceptable level of performance, the compression ratio was increased from 6.25:1, as used in the larger Hudsons, to 6.50:1 for the 112 series.

The result was an engine that was 18 percent smaller than the average of the Big Three low-priced cars, yet it produced comparable horsepower. It would outlive the 112 series, powering the Hudson Traveler and Deluxe series until World War II diverted Hudson's facilities to the manufacture of war materiel.

And as to the basic Hudson splasher six, in its three-inch by five-inch configuration it continued in production through the 1947 model year. It had its critics, right up to the end, yet hundreds of thousands of owners attested to its reliability, durability, and performance, and Hudson aficionados to this day speak of it with both affection and respect!

choice for the job — in order to spotlight the smaller car. Abraham Edward Barit, who had succeeded to the Hudson presidency upon the death of Roy D. Chapin two years earlier, optimistically announced that the firm's plan was to put "men and money back to work." He expected, he said, to double the number of employees to 12,000 and to invest $11 million in tools and production materials.

But as the Scottish poet Robert Burns observed,

> *The best laid plan o' mice an' men*
> *Gang aft a-gley....*

For 1938 was a recession year, a bad one. Hudson production, the new, low-priced series notwithstanding, amounted to less than half of what it had been the year before — the worst, in fact, since 1933, the year that had represented Hudson's nadir. The company's 1938 deficit amounted to more than four-and-a-half million dollars!

Just as Packard had done with its One-Twenty (see *SIA* #47) three years earlier, Hudson named the new 112 for its wheelbase. And despite the high-flown rhetoric put out by the advertising department, there was nothing really new about it at all. Basically the new car was a Terraplane in relatively Spartan trim, mounted on a shorter wheelbase and powered by a de-stroked engine. This is not to suggest that there was anything the matter with the 112. It was a good automobile, and an excellent value for the money, but sensational it wasn't.

In concept the 112 differed sharply from the little Essex Terraplane with which Hudson had attempted, five-and-a-half years earlier, to invade the lowest

Facing page, left: Generously sized cowl vent helps keep passengers cool. **Right:** *Oddly shaped taillamps provide both side and rear illumination. Contemporary Willys used a similar design.* **This page, left:** *Big rear fenders have a quite shallow radius; might have made tire changes a real pain.* **Below:** *112 has twice as many trunk latches as the average car of the time.* **Bottom:** *112 also had its own distinct hubcaps.*

price field. At that time the emphasis had been on performance. This time it was on comfort and economy. And roominess; for the body, from the firewall back, was that of the larger Hudson (and Hudson-Terraplane) models. Passenger accommodations were unusually spacious for a car priced so reasonably. And "low priced" it really was, right down there with the big three, Chevrolet, Ford and Plymouth.

In the interest of fuel economy, the displacement of the six-cylinder Hudson engine, as applied to the Series 112, was cut from 212 cubic inches to 174.9. This was done by the simple expedient of reducing the length of the stroke by seven-eighths of an inch, resulting in the new Hudson having the smallest engine in its price class, apart from Ford's anemic V-8 60 (see *SIA #55*). Studebaker, of course, would come along with a still-smaller engine for its new Champion, but that wouldn't happen for another 15 months (see *SIA #35*).

And so, although Hudson engineers squeezed 83 horsepower out of the little mill (and raised that figure, in 1939, to

86), the 112 was not designed to be a hotshot performer.

Six body styles were offered. A two-door sedan called the brougham (the coach designation having been dropped after 1935), a four-door sedan, a three-passenger coupe, a four-passenger victoria coupe, a three-passenger convertible coupe and a six-passenger convertible brougham. (Hudson had done away with the rumble seat that year, bringing the extra passengers in

Hudson 112 versus the Competition

	Hudson 112	Chevrolet Master Dlx	Ford Deluxe	Plymouth Deluxe	Studebaker Champion Custom
Engine type	L-head 6	Ohv 6	L-head V-8	L-head 6	L-head 6
Horsepower @ rpm	86/4,000	85/3,200	85/3,800	62/3,600	78/4,000
Torque @ rpm	138/1,400	170/2,000	155/2,200	148/1,200	128/1,600
Compression ratio	6.50:1	6.25:1	6.15:1	6.70:1	6.50:1
Main bearings	3	4	3	4	4
Lubrication	Splash	Pressure	Pressure	Pressure	Pressure
Front suspension	Solid axle	Independent	Solid axle	Independent	Independent
Springs (front)	Semi-elliptical	Coil	Transverse	Coil	Transverse
Clutch	Wet, cork inserts	Dry plate	Dry plate	Dry plate	Dry plate
Final drive ratio	4.11:1	4.22:1	3.78:1	4.10:1	4.56:1
Tire size	6.00 x 16	6.00 x 16	6.00 x 16	6.00 x 16	5.50 x 16
Weight*	2,712 pounds	2,875 pounds	2,750 pounds	2,909 pounds	2,375 pounds
Wheelbase	112 inches	112.25 inches	112 inches	114 inches	110 inches
Hp per c.i.d.	.491	.392	.384	.407	.475
Pounds per c.i.d.	15.49	13.27	12.44	14.45	14.46
Pounds per hp	31~53	33.82	32.35	35.47	30.45
Price*	$791	$745	$765	$791	$740

*4-door sedan is used here for purposes of comparison.
Primary source: *Automotive Industries*, November 12, 1938. Other sources also employed.

Right: Plain three-spoke steering wheel has well-defined finger grips. **Below:** Speedo is placed directly in front of driver's position; would be easier to read without the decorative horizontal stripes. **Bottom:** Clock is placed symmetrically in glove box door of wood-grained dash.

1939 HUDSON

out of the weather in the convertible brougham.) The same six body styles were available in the various larger Hudson and Hudson-Terraplane series, providing a proliferation of no fewer than 56 distinct passenger cars, as well as 16 utility and commercial vehicles. Given Hudson's relatively low volume, such a practice seems in retrospect to have made little sense, from the perspective of either the manufacturer or the dealers.

Hudson laid a strong emphasis upon safety in those days. For instance, its

Driving Impressions

Among the motorists who elected to purchase a Hudson 112 in 1939 was Miss Margaret H. Daley, of Oakland, California. Miss Daley selected a black victoria coupe, a neat little four-passenger number with a single transverse-facing occasional seat located behind the driver. This is our driveReport car, and to this day there is a letter in the dashboard compartment, addressed to Miss Daley and postmarked Detroit, Michigan, October 11, 1939. The return address is that of Hudson's vice president in charge of sales, and enclosed is a questionnaire that was to have been returned to that gentleman's office. Obviously, Miss Daley never got around to responding.

As recently as the early 1960s Miss Daley — well along in years by that time — could be seen driving her black Hudson coupe around the streets of Oakland. What happened next is a matter for conjecture, but by 1966 the car — with a hole in the block courtesy of a broken connecting rod — had fallen into the hands of an Alameda teenager. The youngster's intent was to replace the Hudson six with a V-8, turning the little car into a street rod, but fortunately his plans failed to materialize. He sold the car to Hudson collector Bill Lang, who found a used engine for it. A very used engine, as matters turned out, and Lang quickly grew discouraged with the project.

And so, in 1967 Miss Daley's Hudson became the property of Wayne Ballerstein, a Concord, California, transmission shop owner. Wayne has driven Hudsons all his life. He owns a number of them, and even now he makes the 50-mile round trip to the shop, each day, from his home in the village of Isleton, driving a 1952 Hornet brougham! For years, Ballerstein was employed as a mechanic at a succession of Hudson dealerships, and eventually he opened a garage of his own — specializing, of course, in Hudsons. Then, when there weren't enough Hudsons remaining to keep the business solvent, Wayne turned to transmission work

Ballerstein painstakingly rebuilt the weary engine, fitting it with a new crankshaft, new main bearings and the rest. One fender required extensive surgery, but otherwise the body was in good shape, and a new paint job was applied in 1968. It's about due to be painted again, but the original interior is in remarkably good condition — a tribute to the tender loving care the Hudson must have received at the hands of Miss Daley.

For an inexpensive car of the prewar vintage, the seats in this one are remarkably wide and unusually comfortable. Hudson featured deep, foam rubber cushions in 1939, and somehow the foam has retained its shape and resilience over the years. But the hood is high and the driver sits low in relation to it. If Miss Daley happened to be short of stature, she must have had to sit on a cushion in order to see where she was going! Even at six-feet-two we were unable to see the crowns of the Hudson's fenders.

Leg room, however, is ample, and head room is so generous as to lead one to believe that somebody at Hudson must have favored tall hats. In our view, Hudson could have enhanced the car's appearance substantially by shaving an inch or two off its rather considerable height — and without any significant penalty to the Hudson's occupants.

A solenoid beneath the dash activates the engine. Miss Daley would have had to fiddle with a manual choke, but Ballerstein has upgraded the car with a 1946 Hudson carburetor, complete with automatic choke. We let it idle for a few moments to give the splash lubrication system an opportunity to do its job, and then we're under way.

Of all the clutches we've used in 50 years of driving, we like the Hudson's "wet" clutch with its cork inserts best of all. Smooth as cream! Shifts are unexpectedly crisp; the steering column linkage is much less sloppy than the norm. It's easy to clash the gears, however, if one isn't careful. As *The Autocar* explained, "Actual synchromesh is not employed, the gears being of constant-mesh type engaged through dogs — not, of course, the old-style gear-tooth to gear-tooth process. We quickly learned that by shifting a little more slowly, or better yet by double-clutching, clash-free shifts are simple to achieve. Second gear isn't silent, as Hudson liked to claim it to be, but it is quiet and unobtrusive.

Acceleration could hardly be called neck-snapping, but keeping up with traffic poses no problem at all. Out on the freeway we found that the little Hudson seemed happiest at 50 to 55 miles an hour. It manages 60 or better without complaint, but the noise level coming from the engine compartment rises considerably. Wayne Ballerstein observes that in a three-main-bearing engine such as this one, the center main takes a beating at sustained high speeds.

Steering is neither especially light nor heavy. In parking maneuvers it's probably easier to handle than the average 1939 car. It tracks well going down the freeway, but ridges or other irregularities in the pavement telegraph their message straight to the driver's hands.

The Hudson's cornering ability ranks as superior. With characteristic British understatement, *The Autocar* observes, "A torsion bar type of stabiliser links the front axle to the chassis, and it appears that this device has considerable effect in checking roll." Or in plain Yankee talk, this car corners *flat!*

The ride is just a trifle choppy, as one would expect of a relatively short-wheelbase car with a solid front axle. The sensation isn't strong enough to be bothersome, however. As we recall past experiences with other cars of this vintage, we'd be inclined to rate the Hudson 112's ride somewhat better than that of the Ford, though not the equal of either Chevrolet or Plymouth. We had no opportunity to test the Hudson on really steep grades, but its performance on more gentle acclivities was reassuring. We have no doubt that, despite its relatively modest displacement, the 112 would give a satisfactory account of itself in the mountains. On level ground it will start easily from rest in second gear, and it will idle smoothly in high, then gain speed easily without downshifting.

Hudson had pioneered the use of idiot lights back in 1932, and this car employs them for the generator and oil pressure. Temperature and fuel gauges are incorporated into the speedometer dial, and the speedometer itself is an unusual one, its needle moving on a circle eccentric to the circle of the speed calibrations. A wind-up accessory clock is built into the dash compartment door. The presence of an antenna suggests that at one time the car must have been equipped with a radio, but none is in evidence now.

Access to the single rear seat is easier than we expected. Tip the front seat back-rest on the passenger's side and the entire seat rolls forward, providing ample space for boarding. We found the rear seat more comfortable than we anticipated, too, though it was obviously not intended for long-distance travel. The more expensive Hudsons had a second "occasional" seat of the fold-up variety, opposite the fixed-position seat on the left side. But it's apparent that two passengers in that rear compartment would find themselves in very cramped quarters!

The all-steel body feels very solid, and such little touches as the twin latches for the deck lid suggest high-quality construction. The trunk is huge, and there's even a useful little package shelf under the rear window.

The brakes are very effective, stopping the car in a nice, straight line with only minimal pedal pressure. Ballerstein notes that in the 10,000 or so miles that he has driven the 112 he has not observed any tendency for the binders to fade. Even the parking brake, controlled by means of an umbrella handle under the dash, does its job well.

Quite frankly, we liked the Hudson 112 better than we expected to. It's a roomy, comfortable car, a competent performer, and genuinely pleasant to drive. We've never been impressed by the top-heavy styling of the 1936-1940 Hudsons, but the 112, particularly in coupe form, comes off better in that respect than the larger cars.

Gas mileage, so far as we've been able to determine, never really came up to Hudson's expectations, falling generally in the same range as the 112's larger-engined rivals.

But it's a good car, a nice car. And it's not at all difficult to understand why, back in 1939, Miss Margaret Daley chose it over the excellent automobiles being offered by the competition!

illustrations by Russell von Sauers, The Graphic Automobile Studio

© copyright 1984, Special Interest Autos

specifications

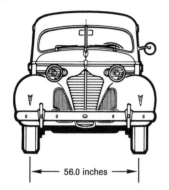

← 56.0 inches →

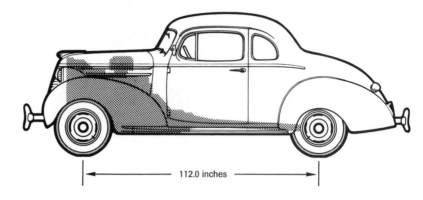

← 112.0 inches →

1939 Hudson 112

Price	$791 f.o.b. factory, with standard equipment
Standard equipment	Front-hinged "safety" hood; front stabilizer; molded foam rubber seat cushion; "draft-free" window vent panes; lockable dash compartment; column-mounted gearshift lever

ENGINE
Type	L-head, 6-cylinder
Bore and stroke	3 inches x 4⅛ inches
Displacement	174.9 cubic inches
Max bhp @ rpm	86 @ 3,000
Max torque @ rpm	138 @ 1,400
Compression ratio	6.50:1
Induction system	Carter downdraft carburetor
Lubrication system	Splash
Electrical system	Auto-Lite 6-volt
Main bearings	3

CLUTCH
Type	Single wet plate, cork inserts
Diameter	8¹¹/₁₆
Actuation	Mechanical, foot pedal

TRANSMISSION
Type	3-speed selective
Ratios: 1st	2.42:1
2nd	1.61:1
3rd	1.00:1
Reverse	2.99:1

DIFFERENTIAL
Type	Spiral bevel
Ratio	4.11:1
Drive axles	Semi-floating

STEERING
Type	Gemmer worm-and roller
Turns lock to lock	4
Ratio	16.4:1
Turn circle	41 feet

BRAKES
Type	Duo-hydraulic with reserve mechanical linkage to rear wheels
Drum diameter	9¹/₁₆
Total braking area	133.2 square inches

CHASSIS & BODY
Frame	X-braced channel section
Body construction	All-steel
Body style	4-passenger victoria coupe

SUSPENSION
Front	Semi-elliptic, longitudinal leaf springs, solid axle
Rear	Semi-elliptic, longitudinal leaf springs, splayed for transverse stability
Tires	6.00 x 16
Wheels	Pressed steel

WEIGHTS AND MEASURES
Wheelbase	112 inches
Overall length	187⅞ inches
Overall height	70½ inches
Overall width	71 inches
Front tread	56 inches
Rear tread	59½ inches
Ground clearance	8 ¹/₁₆
Shipping weight	2,712 pounds

CAPACITIES
Crankcase	6 quarts
Cooling system	12½ quarts
Fuel tank	12½ gallons

PERFORMANCE*
Top speed (av.)	73.32 mph
Acceleration: 0-30	6.2 seconds
0-50	15.7 seconds
0-60	24.8 seconds
Braking distance	30 feet 6 inches @ 30 mph (dry concrete surface)

*Figures from a road test reported by The Autocar, 2/10/39. (The test was conducted using an export model having a compression ratio of 6.25:1 and a horsepower rating of 76. Speed and acceleration figures shown here must therefore be considered to be conservative.)

1939 HUDSON

hydraulic brakes, introduced in the 1936 models, were accompanied by a back-up system which operated the rear binders by means of cables in the event of failure on the part of the hydraulic system. The new 112 series offered another safety feature, one which would be extended the following year to the rest of the Hudson line: The hood was hinged at the front, effectively preventing the possibility of its becoming unlatched and swinging back to block the driver's vision. A lever under the dashboard to the driver's left locked it securely in place.

1939 brought little change to the Hudson 112, apart from an attractive modification of the grille — and four more horsepower. The Terraplane name was dropped that year, replaced by the Hudson Pacemaker and a deluxe version known simply as the Hudson Six, both powered by the Terraplane's 96-horsepower engine. Together with the larger Hudsons, these cars featured headlamps that were recessed into the fenders. The 112 alone clung to the freestanding type. The integral lamps were considered more modish at the time, but to many observers the smaller car, with its orbs flanking the radiator, was better looking.

Prices of the 112 were increased by about five percent for 1939, which was unfortunate, since both Chevrolet and Plymouth were cutting theirs and the tab for a new Ford rose only slightly that year. Nevertheless, Hudson turned out nearly 61 percent more cars than it had produced the year before. Hudson was still losing money, but the deficit was less than a third of what it had been in 1938.

But the Hudson 112 could not be considered a commercial success. By 1940 its place was taken by the slightly larger and marginally more powerful Traveler series, and the Traveler, in turn, had disappeared by the time production resumed following World War II. The smaller Hudsons of the prewar era are rare today, and *SIA* was fortunate to find one in good, original condition to serve as our driveReport subject. ᔆᴽ

Left: In profile the 112 presents an un-remarkable appearance; it's typical late-thirties styling. Below left: Glove compart-ment looks big enough to carry a six-pack. Below center: Side-saddle jump seat is best enjoyed in small doses. Below: Flathead six depended on splash system for lubrication. Bottom left: Split rear win-dow was just becoming passé in 1939.

Acknowledgments and Bibliography
Automotive Industries, *January 8, 1938; October 22, 1938; February 23, 1939; April 1, 1949; Don Butler,* The History of Hudson; *R.M. Clarke (ed.),* Hudson and Railton Cars 1936-1940; *John A Conde,* The Cars That Hudson Built; *Jerry Heasley,* The Production Figure Book for US Cars; *Maurice D. Hendry,* "Hudson," Automobile Quarterly, *Volume IX, No.4; G. Marshall Naul,* The Specification Book for US Cars, 1920-1929; *G. Marshall Naul,* The Specification Book for US Cars, 1930-1969; *Alfred P. Sloan, Jr.,* My Years With Ceneral Motors.
Our thanks to Tom and Lynn Burke, Concord, California; Wayne Graefen, Ful-lerton, California; Roger Henrichs, Con-cord, California; Janet Kale, president, Hudson-Essex-Terraplane Club, Inc., Buena Park, California; Diana McIntyre, Concord, California. Special thanks to Wayne Ballerstein, Isleton, California

Price List: 1939 Hudson

	PRICE	WEIGHT
112 Deluxe Series (112″ w/b, 86 hp)		
Coupe, 3-passenger	$745	2,587 pounds
Victoria Coupe, 4-passenger	$791	2,622 pounds
Touring Brougham	$775	2,682 pounds
Touring Sedan	$806	2,712 pounds
Convertible Coupe, 3-passenger	$886	2,627 pounds
Convertible Brougham, 6-passenger	$936	2,732 pounds
Pacemaker Six, Series 91 (118″ w/b, 96 hp)		
Coupe, 3-passenger	$798	2,717 pounds
Victoria Coupe, 5-passenger	$844	2,752 pounds
Touring Brougham	$823	2,832 pounds
Touring Sedan	$854	2,867 pounds
Hudson Six, Series 92 (118″ w/b, 96 hp)		
Coupe, 3-passenger	$823	2,767 pounds
Victoria Coupe, 5-passenger	$869	2,787 pounds
Touring Brougham	$856	2,847 pounds
Touring Sedan	$898	2,897 pounds
Convertible Coupe, 3-passenger	$972	2,782 pounds
Convertible Brougham, 6-passenger	$1,032	2,892 pounds
Country Club Six, Series 93 (122″ w/b, 101 hp)		
Coupe, 3-passenger	$919	2,848 pounds
Victoria Coupe, 5-passenger	$967	2,893 pounds
Touring Brougham	$960	2,968 pounds
Touring Sedan	$995	3,023 pounds
Convertible Coupe, 3-passenger	$1,052	2,898 pounds
Convertible Brougham, 6-passenger	$1,115	2,983 pounds
Country Club Eight Series 95 (122″ w/b, 122 hp)		
Coupe, 3-passenger	$1,009	3,003 pounds
Victoria Coupe, 5-passenger	$1,051	3,053 pounds
Touring Brougham	$1,049	3,138 pounds
Touring Sedan	$1,079	3,193 pounds
Convertible Coupe, 3-passenger	$1,138	3,033 pounds
Convertible Brougham, 6-passenger	$1,201	3,123 pounds
Custom Country Club Eight, Series 97 (129″ w/b, 122 hp)		
Sedan, 6-passenger	$1,175	3,268 pounds
Sedan, 7-passenger	$1,430	3,378 pounds

That lovable old Bonneville record breaker, the

1940 Hudson 8

driveReport

By Michael Lamm, Editor

HUDSON got its 1940 models off to a blazing start at Bonneville in August 1939. John Cobb, fresh from a new land speed record on the Utah salt (368.85 mph), stepped from the cockpit of his Railton streamliner directly into a brand-new 1940 Hudson 8 sedan. This time he established the International Class C flying kilometer mark for closed cars: 93.89 mph. Later, another 1940 Hudson 8 hit 94.73 mph for the flying five miles.

John Cobb and Hudson factory drivers Al Miller and Buddy Marr racked up no fewer than 102 official AAA Class C and D records for speed and endurance. The runs lasted throughout August and September and into November 1939.

These two Hudsons, equipped with optional rear-axle ratios, overdrive, and high-compression heads (items anyone could get through any Hudson dealer), were completely stock and standard, even to carrying radios and spare tires.

The same Hudson 8 that Cobb had driven also achieved 27.12 mpg in a Bonneville fuel-economy test over a distance of 1,000 miles. In the endurance trials, a 175-cid Hudson 6 sedan covered 30,000 kilometers at 70.62 mph. Another Hudson 6 got 32.66 mpg in the 1,000-mile economy test. In all, it was the greatest such sweep in history — the greatest since a team of 1937 Hudsons and Terraplanes set 40 similar records at Bonneville in October 1936.

The publicity from these runs apparently hit the calculated mark, because suddenly Hudson sales for 1940 took off like a shot. With newspaper publicity and ads ringing out the Bonneville triumphs, showroom sales for the first week of availability were up 125% over the corresponding week in 1939. Hudson had laid off workers a few months before but was now rehiring them to keep up with 1940 demand. The weeks that followed showed even healthier sales gains: 300% the next week for 1940 vs. 1939. Total 1940 September sales beat the same month in 1939 by

149%. Hudson also added 225 new dealers that month. By year's end, Hudson had sold just under 80,000 cars (vs. 62,000 for 1939). Whether the Bonneville records made that big a difference is hard to say, but they plus the 1940 model's new styling added up to what, on the surface, appeared to be a very good year for Hudson.

Elmer Drennon of Santa Clara, Calif., owns a 1940 Hudson 8 sedan that's cherry as a berry and nearly a twin of the Class C record breaker. It lacks only overdrive, the higher c.r., and taller cogs to be identical. Elmer bought this car from its original owner in 1966. The 30-year-old Hockanum Woolen Mills upholstery still looks perfect. It's unblemished and as itchy as ever. Even the Hockanum and Goodyear Airfoam tags are still sewn into the seams. Elmer says the car needed only a touch of rechroming, paint, and a brisk cleanup to bring it back to like-new condition. But those glorious Goodyear wide whites took him two years to find.

We drove the car, and these are our notes: "Extremely solid body. Doors chunk shut with only the lightest tug or shove. High, upright seats, Airfoam soft, good both front and rear. Rearward vision fair, otherwise good. Clean, handsome dash design. Miss gauges, though; dislike idiot lights, especially oil and amps way over there on the glovebox.

"Car starts quickly, with characteristic Hudson ching-a-ling starter sound. Engine idles with great smoothness. No synchro on any gear makes engaging low the wait-a-minute sort. Very smooth clutch. Wet. Cork-lined disc runs in oil. Ah, yes.

"Pickup is brisk but not whiplashing. Love that gear whine in low. Crunch to second. More gear whine, but not so noticeable in second. Crunch to high. Purrs along like a refrigerator. Light, precise steering.

Centerpoint excellent. Ride harsher than most modern cars, but why not? Stabilizer bars do their jobs. No wallow, no sudden shifting of body after the wheels have been cocked. Brakes seem great, bring car down quickly. Good pedal feel." (We drove mostly through the coastal mountain range south of San Francisco, along country roads, and then around Stanford University, spending most of the day behind the wheel.)

For 1940, Hudson offered the 175-cid splasher 6, a 212-cid Super Six (also a splasher), and the old splasher 8 we were driving. By "splasher" we mean the rod bearings, cam, valves, wrist pins, and cylinder walls were lubricated by dippers on the con-rod caps. There was an oil pump, but about all it did was refill the oil supply in the dipper troughs. Dry, the 8's pan took nine quarts of oil, but in an oil change, you added only seven, the other two staying in the troughs. After splashing around, the oil drained down to the mains. In other words, the mains were gravity lubricated. The venerable Hudson 8 kept this oiling system from its birth in 1930 through its retirement in 1952. Everyone but the Hudson factory called it the "dipper" or "splasher" system. Hudson called it Duo-Flo lubrication.

All three 1940 Hudson engines used the same 3-inch bore, an economy move that made pistons interchangeable. The small 6 had a 4.125-inch stroke for 175 cid and 92 bhp at 4,000 mm. The Super Six was nearly identical except for a 5-inch stroke (212 cid and 102 bhp). Finally, the 8, with 254 cubes, churned up 128 bhp at 4,200 rpm. All were flatheads, of course, and all would rev high and long without complaint.

Hudson dropped the Terraplane tag after 1938 and added the Hudson 112 line. This spanned a 112-inch wheelbase and cost just a few dollars more than Chev/Ford/Plymouth. In 1940, they added an inch

Graceful hulk of 1940 Hudson 8 flashes by as it did 30 years ago in Utah to establish no fewer than 102 AAA speed records.

In 1940-41, buyers could order Hudsons with or without running boards. All models were over-engineered, well crafted.

Elegant, uncluttered dashboard unfortunately uses idiot lights but has 2 ashtrays, big glovebox. Interior of the test car is all original, including radio, which plays as well as any new transistor.

The Goodyear tag is still intact on front seat, as is another tag from Hockanum Woolen Mills.

Big splasher 8 puts out 128 bhp, survived from 1930 through 1952, hooks to non-synchro 3-speed transmission. Record breakers used o.d.

Stabilizer bars front and rear give almost no lean on corners. Hudson's Auto-Poise suspension plus center-point steering aid good handling.

Amazingly deep, tall trunk has bin near lid to carry tools. Spare takes up little room.

Hudson's "wet" clutch disc had cork facings (like soda-bottle corks) running in thin oil.

Frank Spring, top Hudson stylist, believed in keeping frills functional, discreet, and tasteful.

1940 Hudson driveReport

to the 112's wheelbase and called the lowest-priced series Traveler. Also on the 113-inch wheelbase were the Business 6 and Deluxe. Next came the Super Six and the Hudson 8 on a 118-inch wheelbase. Finally, the Big Boy 6 and the posh Country Club series (in either Super Six or 8) spanned 125 inches. Not many Country Clubs were sold, a pity because these amounted to factory semi-customs.

The Country Club 4-door's extra length came by using coupe doors up front. Most of the additional seven inches, though, were taken up by the thickness of the front seatback, so there was barely more leg room in the Country Club than in a standard 4-door 8. Yet this seat-back did contain a pull-open compartment for briefcases or refreshments. Also, this series' 2-tone Hockanum and/or leather upholstery and appointments were far more luxurious than any other 1940 Hudson's. Chrome trim, rolls, pleats, depth of cushioning and carpets—these and much more enhanced the Country Club's interior. Outwardly, the only signs of its higher station were the longer look, small Country Club insignia on its nose, and a split front bumper a la Zephyr.

You could order the 1940 (and even the 1941) Hudson with or without running boards. It cost no more either way. 1940 marked the first year for Hudson's independent coil spring front suspension. This mounted tubular

hydraulic shocks inside the springs and had a rubber-bushed front stabilizer bar, introduced with 1939 models and called Auto-Poise, as standard equipment. Although stabilizers very much like Hudson's had been used before on any number of cars, Auto-Poise differed from other torsional stabilizers in that the links were connected to the front-wheel backing plates, putting more torsion on the bar the tighter the turn. Hudson also used a lateral rear stabilizer bar beginning in 1940 and took out a basic patent on Auto-Poise that year.

The Super Six and 8 got vacuum spark advance for 1940 and continued dual-throat carbs with automatic choke, automatic heat control, and simultaneous accelerator jets. Transmission ratios were changed to make better use of the three engines' torque curves. Electric Hand pre-selector shifting got bumped that year, but you could order automatic overdrive with tiptoe control, "Fluid Cushioned" automatic clutch, or both together.

Brakes continued the Triple Safe feature Hudson had pioneered in 1936. The main system was conventional hydraulic, but if any line broke, pushing the brake pedal nearly to the floor engaged a mechanical reserve braking system. This consisted of the hand-brake cables to the rear wheels.

The 1940 Hudson proved a solidly engineered, well crafted, handsomely styled car—right for its day, comfortable, reasonably fast, very roadable, reasonably priced.

The AAA records, while current, *were* talked about. Yet despite all the honors and increased sales that came Hudson's way in 1940, the company closed out the year with a net loss of over $1.5 million. ☙

John Cobb, his Railton Red Lion, and the 1940 Hudson 8 in Utah, 1939.

Our thanks to 1940 Hudson owner Elmer Drennon of Santa Clara, Calif.; to John Conde, American Motors Corp.; and to the Hudson-Essex-Terraplane club, 18829 Valerio St., Reseda, California.

AAA Contest Board American Stock Car Records

Closed Car Div,. Class C (183-305) & Class D (122-183 cid)

DISTANCE			SPEED. MPH 1940 HUDSON 8	SPEED. MPH 1940 HUDSON 6
1	K	S	------	48.39
1	M	S	------	54.68
5	K	S	82.89	67.71
5	M	S	86.40	71.29
10	K	S	86.28	73.07
10	M	S	87.93	73.11
1	K	F	93.89	81.19
1	M	F	93.88	81.19
5	K	F	94.73	81.19
5	M	F	94.73	81.19
10	K	F	94.73	81.19
10	M	F	92.89	81.18
25	K	F	93.64	80.06
25	M	F	93.66	80.14
50	K	F	93.71	80.19
50	M	F	93.68	80.39
75	K	F	93.68	80.36
75	M	F	93.69	80.51
100	K	F	93.70	80.45
100	M	F	93.67	80.63
200	K	F	92.39	70.86
200	M	F	92.73	70.41
250	K	F	92.56	70.61
250	M	F	92.29	70.42
300	K	F	92.68	70.42
300	M	F	92.49	70.42
400	K	F	92.28	70.42
400	M	F	92.54	70.42
500	K	F	92.54	70.24
500	M	F	92.42	70.31
1,000	K	F	91.87	70.29
1,000	M	F	91.34	70.40
2,000	K	F	88.57	70.36
2,000	M	F	87.78	70.46
3,000	K	F	87.88	70.47
3,000	M	F	------	70.32
4,000	K	F	------	70.59
4,000	M	F	------	70.48
5,000	K	F	------	70.36
5,000	M	F	------	70.56
10,000	K	F	------	70.62
10,000	M	F	------	70.67
15,000	K	F	------	70.73
15,000	M	F	------	70.68
20,000	K	F	------	70.71
20,000	M	F	------	70.58
25,000	K	F	------	70.66
30,000	K	F	------	70.62
1 hr.			93.68	80.54
3 hr.			92.41	70.41
6 hr.			92.12	70.44
12 hr.			91.29	70.36
24 hr.			87.68	70.45
2 days			------	70.41
3 days			------	70.58
4 days			------	70.65
5 days			------	70.72
6 days			------	70.68
7 days			------	70.71
8 days			------	70.72
9 days			------	70.68
10 days			------	70.68
11 days			------	70.62
12 days			------	70.58

NOTE: 1 K S means One Kilometer Standing; 75 M F means 75 Miles Flying, etc.

SPECIFICATIONS
1940 Hudson 8 4-door sedan (Model 44)

price when new ....$952 fob. Detroit (1940).
Current valuation ....Xlnt $1620; gd. $600.

ENGINE
    Type ....In-line, L-head 8. cast en bloc, water-cooled. 5 mains.
    Bore & stroke ....3.00 x 4.50 in.
    Displacement ....254.4 cu. in.
    Max. bhp @ rpm ....128 @ 4,200.
    Max. torque @ rpm ....198 @ 1,600.
    Compression ratio ....6.5:1.
    Induction system ....Carter 2-bbl. downdraft carb.
    Exhaust system ....Cast-iron manifold, single exhaust pipe & muffler.
    Electrical system ....6-volt battery/coil (Autolite).

CLUTCH
    Type ....Single wet plate, cork facings run in oil.
    Disc diameter ....10.0 in.
    Actuation ....Mechanical, foot pedal.

TRANSMISSION
    Type ....3-speed manual, column lever.
    Ratios: 1st ....2.42:1.
    2nd ....1.60:1.
    3rd ....1.00:1.
    Reverse ....2.99:1.

DIFFERENTIAL
    Type ....Hypoid, spiral bevel gears.
    Ratio ....4.11:1.
    Drive axles ....Semi-floating.

STEERING
    Type ....Worm & roller.
    Ratio ....18.2:1.
    Turns lock to lock ....4.5.
    Turn circle ....42.2 ft.

BRAKES
    Type .... 4-wheel drums, hydraulic. internal expanding, with mechanical safety cables on rear.
    Drum diameter ....11.0625 in.
    Total swept area ....255.7 sq. in.

CHASSIS & BODY
    Frame ....Channel-section steel, X-member.
    Body ....All steel.
    Front Suspension ....Independent. unequal A-arms, coil springs, tubular hydraulic shocks.
    Rear Suspension ....Solid axle. Semi-elliptical longitudinal sprinqs, tubular shocks, anti-sway bar.
    Tires ....6.00 x 16, 4-ply, tube type.
    Wheels ....Pressed-steel bolt-ons.

WEIGHTS & MEASURES
    Wheelbase ....118.0 in.
    Front tread .... 56.25 in.
    Rear tread ....59.50 in.
    Overall length ....195.375 in.
    Overall height ....70.5 in.
    Overall width .... 72.0 in.
    Ground clearance .... 8.44 in.
    Curb weight ....3185 lb.

CAPACITIES
    Crankcase ....7.0 qt.
    Cooling system ....18 5 qt.
    Gas tank ....16.5 gal.

* Courtesy **Antique Automobile Appraisal.**

1946 HUDSON SUPER SIX

Originally published in Special Interest Autos #72, Nov.-Dec. 1982

Hudson's Postwar Success

by Arch Brown
photos by Jim Janji

Above: As with most 1946 cars, Hudson's body shell was carried over from 1942 models. Left: Low windshield gives Hudson convert a speedy appearance but makes overhead traffic lights hard to see. Below: Hudson stylists did a nice job with '46 facelift; gave car a low, wide appearance.

HUDSON MARCHED to a different drummer. Always did. As early as 1911—only a year after the first Hudson appeared—the car had an oil-cushioned, cork-insert clutch. And 43 years later, when the last Detroit-built Hudson (an aficionado would say the last *real* Hudson) came down the line, a refined version of that same "wet" clutch was still being used.

There were other—well, *peculiarities.* Splash lubrication was employed long after everyone else had gone to full pressure: until 1948 in the six-cylinder cars, and right up to the end in the straight-eights. The competition derided it, but Hudson made it work.

There were odd features like the "pinned" piston rings, and an engine block so hard it could ruin a boring bar if the machinist didn't know what he was doing. (Not that one had to rebore a Hudson very often!) And there were "Duo-Automatic" brakes, in which mechanical action took over in the event of a hydraulic failure.

Even the inside door locks were unconventional. In a Hudson you *pulled up* on the little knob in order to fasten the lock. Everyone else's car, then as now, required that you *push down* to lock up. The Hudson system may have been confusing, but it was not without merit. It's pretty hard for a thief to open a door with a piece of wire if he has to press down on the lock!

But we're getting ahead of the story. To trace the Hudson to its inception we must go back to the Olds Motor Works, in the early years of the century. Ransom

Right: This has to be one of the very best-looking early postwar US convertibles. Below: In contrast to gobs of trim in the front, it's used sparingly in the rear.

1946 HUDSON

E. Olds had assembled a formidable array of talent. Young talent. The group included Roy Chapin (see sidebar, p. 55); Howard Coffin, rising genius of the engineering staff; Fred Bezner in the purchasing department; and Jim Brady, who in 1901 had literally saved the company when he pushed the prototype Curved-Dash Runabout to safety, the day the plant burned down.

Ransom Olds may have been the company's founder, but he was by no means in charge of the store. His financial backers had the final say, and what they said didn't sound good to Olds. They proposed to move the Oldsmobile out of the low-priced field, where it had been the dominant marque, and take up the manufacture of large, powerful and expensive machines. Olds, enraged at the way things were going, pulled out and founded the REO Motor Car Company—named, of course, for his own initials.

Howard Coffin, meanwhile, had devoted himself to the development of a medium-priced car which he hoped would provide an acceptable compromise between the modest ambitions of the founder and the high-flying plans of the Board of Directors. The powers that be vetoed Coffin's design, however, and for the 1906 season Oldsmobile offered essentially the same big car as the year before. The fast-selling little runabout was phased out, and Olds sales faltered badly.

It was at this point that Chapin, Coffin, Bezner and Brady struck off on their own. Seeking capital with which to build the new car that Howard Coffin had designed, Roy Chapin approached E.R. Thomas, manufacturer of the famed, Buffalo-based Thomas Flyer. The result was the Thomas-Detroit, priced—at $2,750—to complement the more expensive "Flyer."

The metamorphosis of the Thomas Detroit into the Chalmers and eventually—broadly speaking—into the Chrysler is a story in itself. But meanwhile, Chapin and Coffin, in company with two other Olds alumni, Roscoe Jackson and George Dunham, had in mind the idea of building a thousand-dollar automobile,

And so the Hudson Motor Car Company was organized early in 1909, as a spinoff of what had become known by that time as Chalmers-Detroit. The Hudson name was that of a Detroit department store magnate who—evidently importuned by his niece, who was married to Roscoe Jackson—provided most of the $15,000 "start-up" capital for the venture. J.L. Hudson's presidency of the new company was apparently no more than titular. In less than a year Roy Chapin, who appears to have been the driving force behind the operation from the beginning, was officially in charge.

The first Hudson automobile, introduced in mid-1909 as a 1910 model, was a jaunty little 100-inch-wheelbase roadster, advertised at $900. It was strictly an "assembled" car. Most cars were in those days; and the Hudson

Hudson Price Comparison Chart
1946 compared with corresponding 1941 and 1942 models

Series	Body Style	Weight (1946)	Price (1946)	Price (1942)	Price (1941)
Super Six	Coupe, 3-passenger	2950	$1481	$1036	$881
	Club coupe	3015	$1553	$1090	$926
	Brougham	3030	$1511	$1064	$901
	Sedan	3085	$1555	$1092	$932
	Convertible brougham	3195	$1879	$1332	$1155
Super Eight	Club Coupe	3185	$1664	$1215	$1040
	Sedan	3235	$1668	$1223	$1039
Commodore Six	Club Coupe	3065	$1693	$1175	$997
	Sedan	3150	$1699	$1181	$994
Commodore Eight	Club Coupe	3235	$1760	$1215	$1030
	Sedan	3305	$1774	$1223	$1029
	Convertible Brougham	3410	$2050	$1451	$1254

If nothing else, the above table demonstrates that inflation is not a new phenomenon!

Left: How to visually lower a rather high hood line: use a couple lines of horizontal trim to bring your eye down to the main part of the body. Below: typically unusual Hudson feature is the forward-opening hood. Remember the big deal Ford made about this development in 1957 when they "introduced" it on their cars?

a good one. Its L-head four came from the Atlas Engine Works, its transmission from Buda, and other components from sundry manufacturers. Its makers claimed a top speed of at least 50 miles an hour, a very brisk pace for an inexpensive car in those days.

By the time 1910 rolled around Hudson had cut its ties with Chalmers-Detroit, standing thenceforth as a separate (and for many years privately held) corporation. J.L. Hudson became chairman of the board, with Chapin as president, Jackson as treasurer and general manager, and Coffin as chief engineer.

At the end of its first full year of production Hudson stood in seventeenth place industry-wide, a remarkable achievement at a time when there were literally hundreds of makes on the market. By this time Buda was Hudson's principal engine supplier, Hudson production having outstripped the capacity of the tiny Atlas organization. (Buda, in turn, would be supplanted a year later by Continental. Not until 1916 would Hudson design and produce its own engines.)

Somewhat more expensive than the original Hudson, the 1911 model was a larger, more powerful car; and in 1912 both price and power were advanced again. By now Hudson had a car that would readily do a mile a minute—at a price nearly double that of the company's initial offering.

But Chapin, Coffin et al were never content with the status quo. Noting the increasing popularity of six-cylinder engines among the luxury marques, they determined to build a six at a more modest price. The first such Hudson was introduced for the 1913 season. It was a fairly large car, with performance that rivaled that of machines which commanded nearly double its price. A year later a smaller "six" was introduced,

1946 Comparison Chart
Medium-Priced Convertible Coupes

	Hudson Super 6	Hudson Commodore 8	Buick Super	Chrysler Windsor	De Soto Custom	Mercury	Oldsmobile 66
Price (fob)	$1879	$2050	$2046	$1861	$1761	$1711	$1681
Weight	3195	3410	4050	3693	3618	3340	3605
Number of cylinders	6	8	8	6	6	8	6
Bore/Stroke	3" x 5"	3" X 4-1/2"	3-3/32" X 4-1/8"	3-7/16" x 4-1/2"	3-7/16" X 4-1/2"	3-3/16" x 3-3/4"	3-1/2" x 4-1/8"
Displacement (cid)	212.0	254.0	248.0	250.6	236.6	239.4	238.1
Compression ratio	6.5:1	6.5:1	6.3:1	6.6:1	6.6:1	6.75:1	6.5:1
Bhp @ rpm	102/4000*	128/4200*	110/3600	114/3600	109/3600	100/3800	100/3400
Torque @ rpm	168/1200*	193/1600*	206/2000	204/1200	192/1200	180/2000	190/1200
Lubrication system	Splash	Splash	Pressure	Pressure	Pressure	Pressure	Pressure
Final drive ratio	4.11:1	4.11:1	4.45:1	3.90:1	3.90:1	3.54:1	4.30:1
Braking area	138.9	141.2	161.5	173.5	173.5	168.0	159.8
Tire size	6.00 x 16	6.50 x 15	6.50 x 16	6.50 x 15	6.50 x 15	6.50 x 15	6.50 x 16
Wheelbase	121 inches	121"	124"	121-1/2"	121-1/2"	118"	119"
Overall length	207-3/8 inches	207-3/8"	212-3/8"	208-1/4"	207-1/4"	201-3/4"	204"

*Hudson's figures for horsepower and torque are shown with standard accessories; other makes are shown without. This amounts to about a five percent penalty for Hudson's horsepower figures, and a two-three percent difference in the torque. It was Hudson's custom to show their figures in this manner.

Hudson dash is attractive, with its sunken radio speaker, but the idiot lights for oil and generator are more than a trifle impractical; they're mounted 'way over by the glove compartment.

and never again would the Hudson name appear on a four-cylinder automobile. By 1915 Hudson was able to bill itself as "the world's largest manufacturer of six-cylinder cars," and its output ranked the car in sixth place for the year.

The title "Super Six," so long associated with Hudson, was first applied to the company's 1916 model, the first to feature a Hudson-built engine. It was a powerplant well in advance of its time, squeezing 76 horsepower out of the same displacement as the 48-horsepower Continental which it replaced. A string of performance records followed, both on the racetracks and in hill-climbing contests.

Predictably, Hudson sales doubled that year!

The company's next major move was the introduction of the Essex, in 1919. By that time the Hudson fetched a price well in excess of $2000, and the creation of a lower-priced companion car seemed a prudent move. That first Essex was a stout, F-head four-banger priced at $1345; hardly a cheap car! The severe recession of 1921-22 forced a reduction in that figure, and in the price of the Hudson as well.

Late In 1921 the Essex began to feature a two-door, five-passenger closed car called the coach, priced only $300 above the touring car. At a time when closed cars typically commanded a very high price, this was a major step; and within a few months the company topped its own act with a $250 price cut. Not only did Essex sales quickly eclipse those of the Hudson, but the trend was set for the entire industry. The closed car had arrived!

In 1924 Essex did it again: a six-cylinder car at a four-cylinder price, only $950 for the coach. Smoother than the

four but a good deal less powerful, as originally designed the Essex "six" was fraught with problems (see *SIA* #38). Its engine, which displaced only 129.9 cubic inches (compared to 180 in the "four") was overworked, and rod bearings were a frequent casualty.

By 1927 Hudson and Essex between them held 8-1/2 percent of the automobile market, with the Essex outselling its parent almost three to one. Hudson had a fine new F-head engine that year, but it was the Essex engine—enlarged and improved by then—that would be of lasting significance. For that little L-head was the direct ancestor of the

engine in our driveReport Hudson, built nearly 20 years later!

1929 was a heady year for the automobile industry, and certainly for the Hudson Motor Car Company. Total sales came to 298,665 cars, which proved to be the company's all-time high; and the Essex was in third place behind Ford and Chevrolet. But there were already signs of trouble. Profits, which had peaked at more than $21 million in 1925, had been falling steadily and now stood at $11.5 million; and Hudson's market penetration was down to 6.6 percent.

The coming of the Depression in 1930 brought still more trouble. Profits were

Hudson Calendar Year Production
1910-1957
(Including Essex and Terraplane)

Year	Production	Year	Production
1910	4445	1933	40,982
1911	6486	1934	85,835
1912	5708	1935	101,080
1913	6401	1936	123,266
1914	10,261	1937	111,342
1915	12,864	1938	51,078
1916	25,772	1939	82,161
1917	20,976	1940	79,979
1918	12,526	1941	79,529
1919	40,054	1942	5396
1920	45,937	1945	5005
1921	27,143	1946	93,870
1922	64,464	1947	100,393
1923	88,914	1948	142,454
1924	133,950	1949	142,462
1925	269,474	1950	143,586
1926	227,508	1951	92,859
1927	276,414	1952	79,117
1928	282,203	1953	67,089
1929	300,962	1954	32,293
1930	113,898	1955	52,688
1931	57,825	1956	22,588
1932	57,550	1957	4080

Source: Jerry Heasley, *The Production Figure Book for US Cars*

virtually wiped out, and four straight years of heavy losses lay just ahead.

But 1930 also brought a change of direction for Hudson. "Straight-eight" engines had become the vogue, and Hudson introduced one that year, replacing the heavy, expensive and virtually indestructible Super Six. This was the Great Eight, and it was nothing more nor less than the Essex engine with two more cylinders added. A distinguished piece of machinery it was not, but it was cheap to produce—and it worked. Smaller and a good deal less powerful than the six it replaced, its performance was adequate only because nearly 600 pounds had been cut from the car's weight.

The Hudson Super Six reappeared in 1933, using the engine of what had become known by then as the Essex Terraplane. (The Essex name was dropped altogether the following year.) And so, on through 1947 all Hudson automobiles were powered by engines derived from that of the Essex. Drivers of mountain roads, especially, deplored the loss of the old F-head's fantastic torque; but the move made the Hudson more price-competitive than before.

Prosperity returned to the depression-ridden automobile industry in 1940-41. Sales of new cars increased dramatically. Even some of the independents, notably Studebaker and Nash, were experiencing a marked up-turn in both sales and profits. Not so with Hudson, whose sales actually fell during this period. In fact, production in 1940 was a full 26 percent below the figure of four years earlier; and the company lost 1.5 million dollars.

It's not that Hudson wasn't trying. Throughout the prewar years the company maintained its presence in the low-priced field, first with the Terraplane, then the Hudson 112 (named for its wheelbase, same as that of the Ford), and finally with the handsome Traveler. All were priced within $25 or so of the "low-priced three," and all offered a lot of automobile for the money. But buyers were not impressed in sufficient numbers to make it a profitable endeavor.

The coming of World War II brought burgeoning prosperity to many—perhaps most—manufacturing concerns, in and out of the automobile industry. Hudson turned to the building of marine engines, aircraft components, and guns. Yet the company's profits were modest, only about half the figure of 1941 and a small fraction of the peak times of the mid-twenties. Thus Hudson, unlike most of its competitors, failed to build up a large cash reserve as the result of its wartime activities.

At war's end Hudson was among the first to resume automobile production, with its 1946 models coming off the assembly line at the end of August 1945. Hudson—or anyone else at that point—could sell as many cars as the factory could turn out; but unfortunately, allocations of sheet steel and other critical materials were based upon the companies' respective output in the immediate prewar years, a period which had not been a good one for Hudson. Consequently, production totals were much lower than the company (and the public) might have wished.

Given this restriction in output, Hudson wisely chose not to re-introduce its less expensive cars during this period, concentrating instead upon the more profitable Super and Commodore Sixes and Eights. Mechanically unchanged from their prewar counterparts, their styling was distinguished by an attractive new recessed grille.

This, then, is our driveReport car: the 1946 Hudson Super Six. Virtually a 1941 model, as though time had stood still for five years—which in a sense it had—it's a car of proven design and attractive lines.

Hudson went on, of course, to introduce a totally new car in 1948, a car that featured a "monobilt" body of step-down design, dramatic new styling, and a brand-new six-cylinder engine (the largest six then available in a production car) with, for the first time on a Hudson, full-pressure lubrication.

Driving Impressions

No group of owners is more fiercely loyal than the Hudson crowd. Tom Burke and his father Melvin (universally known as "Red") are cases in point. Between them they own seven Hudsons, six in operating order and one presently undergoing surgery. Their association with the marque is a long one, Red having run a Hudson garage during Tom's growing-up years.

Rarest of all the Burkes' Hudsons is this deep red 1946 Super Six convertible brougham. A lot of hand work went

illustrations by Russell von Sauers, The Graphic Automobile Studio

specifications

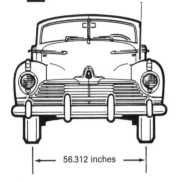

56.312 inches

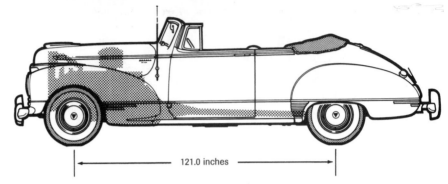

121.0 inches

1946 Hudson Super Six

Price	$1879 fob factory, with standard equipment
Optional equipment on driveReport car	Radio, heater, overdrive, deluxe steering wheel, turn signals, clock, 15-inch wheels

ENGINE
Type	6-cylinder in-line, L-head
Bore & stroke	3-inch x 5-inch
Displacement	212 cubic inches
Max bhp @ rpm	102 @ 4000 with standard accessories
Taxable horsepower	21.6
Max torque @ rpm	168 @ 1200 with standard accessories
Compression ratio	6.5:1
Main bearings	3
Induction system	Carter 1-inch dual downdraft carburetor
Lubrication system	Splash
Electrical system	Auto-Lite, 6-volt

CLUTCH
Type	Fluid cushioned, cork-insert disc
Diameter	10 inches (with overdrive); 8 11/16 inches standard
Actuation	Mechanical, foot pedal

TRANSMISSION
Type	3-speed selective, helical gears. Constant-mesh second; synchronized second and third gears
Ratios: 1st	2.88:1
2nd	1.82:1
3rd	1:1
Reverse	3.50:1

DIFFERENTIAL
Type	Spiral bevel
Ratio	4.55:1 (with overdrive; 4.11:1 standard)
Drive axles	Semi-floating

STEERING
Type	Gemmer worm-and-roller
Turns lock to lock	4½
Ratio (gear)	18.2:1
Turning radius	21.3 feet

BRAKES
Type	Bendix "Duo-Automatic"
Drum diameter	10 inches
Total swept area	138.9 square inches

CHASSIS & BODY
Frame	7⅜-inch siderails, 1¾-inch flanges, ⅛-inch thickness
Body construction	All-steel, body-on-frame
Body style	5-passenger convertible brougham

SUSPENSION
Front	Independent, coil springs
Rear	60-inch x 1¾-inch semi-elliptical leaf springs
Shock absorbers	Monroe, 2-way
Tires	6.50 x 15 (6.00 x 16 standard)
Wheels	5 x 15 (4.5 x 16 standard)

WEIGHTS AND MEASURES
Wheelbase	121 inches
Overall length	207.385 inches
Overall height	68.75 inches (top up)
Overall width	72.75 inches
Front tread	56.312 inches
Rear tread	59.5 inches
Ground clearance	8.375 inches
Shipping weight	3195 pounds

CAPACITIES
Crankcase	4.5 quarts
Cooling system	13 quarts
Fuel tank	16.5 gallons

into the construction of the convertible bodies, which were derived from the shell of the club coupe with additional bracing provided in the quarter panels. So it's not surprising that only a comparative handful were built.

When Tom found the car In 1974 it had been stored for a number of years. Complete and basically sound, it needed a total restoration. Red undertook the job, starting in 1978, with Tom in the role of "gofer." The work took four years to complete.

It's not intended to be a "show" car, though It's not far off the mark. Tom and his family prefer, instead, to drive it and enjoy it. Nevertheless, it was displayed at the 1982 Silverado Concours d'Elegance. It didn't win a trophy, but it turned a lot of heads.

There are a number of unique features to this automobile; the forward-hinged hood, for instance. It's a great safety feature; no danger of a poorly latched bonnet popping up in your face. It's a long hood, providing plenty of room to accommodate the extra length of the engine in the eight-cylinder models.

One of the neatest tricks is the way the front seat slides forward when the backrest is tipped, facilitating entry to the rear seat. The light switch is another indication of Hudson's individuality. It's a large plastic button on the dashboard. Push it once and the parking lights come on. Another poke and the headlights are illuminated. Once more and it's Lights Out.

The turn-signal control is different, too. There's no stalk protruding from the steering column. Instead, beneath the wheel, mounted on the under-side of the column is a set of three buttons:

one for right signal, one for left, and the middle button to cancel the flasher. We're too absent-minded to deal with such a device, or perhaps just spoiled by today's self-cancelling mechanisms. At any rate, we found ourselves reverting instinctively to the old-time hand signals.

The starter is activated by another big plastic button, similar to the one that controls the lights; and the engine comes quickly (and surprisingly quietly) to life. It's tight, having been run only a few hundred miles since it was bored and balanced.

The clutch engages smoothly; there's nothing gentler than the Hudson "wet" clutch if it's properly maintained. Shifts are easy; the column linkage works more smoothly than some we've tried. Acceleration is on the leisurely side. Performance buffs, back in 1946, would

Body styling is pleasantly rounded without appearing bulbous.

have heen well-advised to opt for the eight-cylinder engine.

This Hudson's steering wheel is the optional job that came as standard equipment only on the upscale Commodore series. It's huge, larger in diameter than the regular Super series wheels. And the steering is one of the car's best qualities. It turns easily and not as slowly as we had anticipated. Bumps are effectively cushioned, and the car runs true.

Springing is soft, making for a comfortable ride under most conditions.

But it will "bottom out" on deep dips, and at times there's more bounce than we like—a new set of shock absorbers notwithstanding.

Traveling down the expressway, we drop the Hudson into overdrive. Engine noise, never obtrusive in this car, is reduced even further; the sensation is almost one of gliding! The car is really at its best here, maintaining an easy cruising speed of 55 or 60. Tom reports it's a little slow in the mountains, though it never overheats.

Coming into the downtown area, we notice that the sharply vee'd windshield is positioned in such away that it is almost impossible to see the overhead traffic lights. The seat is fairly high, contributing somewhat to this situation.

The Hudson-Zenith radio embodies a feature that we particularly like. A footswitch changes it, successively, to five different stations. Or, if the button is depressed gently, the device can be used to silence the radio during commercial breaks.

The brakes, we find, do a good job of hauling the Hudson up short. Provided, that is, one leans on the pedal. Hard! Power brakes would be a real boon to this car.

Just to see what it was like, we climbed into the rear seat. Didn't stay long, however. There's plenty of room back there for Tom and Lynn Burke's two daughters, Megan (5-1/2) and

Roy D. Chapin

"There's a general feeling of optimism in the air," declared Roy D. Chapin the day he was sworn in as President Hoover's Secretary of Commerce. "You can almost reach out and touch it, it's that tangible.... It appears the Depression has run its course. The upturn has come. We go ahead in spurts. It's time to spurt again—this time to new levels of prosperity, based on a foundation more stable than ever before!"

This was Chapin, the consummate politician, talking. He understood his role in the faltering Hoover administration. Chapin, the respected businessman, knew better. It was August 1932, and the economy was in the pits. Chapin's own organization, the Hudson Motor Car Company, was on its way to losing five and a half million dollars for the year, and prospects for improvement were bleak.

Chapin's career in the automobile industry had begun 31 years earlier when, at the age of 21 he was hired by the Olds Motor Works as a test driver. Perhaps his considerable skill as a photographer helped him land the job; in any event, he was responsible for the pictures in the company's very first catalog.

Some goodly notoriety came to Roy Chapin in October 1901, when he was selected to drive one of the tiny, one-cylinder Oldsmobile curved-dash runabouts from Detroit to New York—something never before attempted. The 860-mile trip, which required seven days to complete, generated

no end of publicity for the company, and the orders began to pour in. Soon Oldsmobile was the best-selling car in the industry; and by 1904 Chapin—only 24 years of age—was the organization's sales manager.

Roy Chapin went on—as recounted in the accompanying article—to become one of the founders, first of the E.R. Thomas-Detroit Company and then, in 1909, of Hudson. Within a year he was president of the latter concern, although he was but 30 years of age at the time. Thirteen years later he stepped up to the position of chairman of the board.

World War I found Chapin serving his country as chairman of the Highways Transportation Committee, responsible for the shipment of munitions and men to embarcation points.

A strong advocate of better roads, and incidentally a superb public speaker, Chapin in the postwar years was one of the organizers of the Lincoln Highway Association. In 1924 he helped develop the Pan American Federation for Highway Education, serving as a member of its executive committee. Three years later he was appointed chairman of the newly created World Transport Committee, in Paris. In recognition of his service as president of the International Road Congress, held in Washington in 1930, he was made an officer of the French Legion of Honor. He also served as chairman of the highways transport committee of the

National Automobile Chamber of Commerce, predecessor of the Automobile Manufacturers Association.

In 1933, with his company—along with the rest of the industry—in deep trouble, Roy Chapin once again became Hudson's president, responsible for the active management of the company's affairs. By 1935, doubtless in part because of a slight improvement in the economy but also in considerable measure as the result of Chapin's management skills, Hudson was once again turning a profit. *Newsweek* magazine, in a thumbnail sketch published that year, said of him, "Today at 55, Chapin looks 45—unpaunched, easy-smiling, and graying only at the temples. Cameras, the love of his youth, are still a passion. At his Grosse Pointe Farms home he snaps innumerable stills and movie films of his wife and their six children." (The eldest of the six, Roy D. Chapin Jr., went on to hold a number of important posts with Hudson, and ultimately to become chairman of the company's successor, American Motors Corporation.)

But time was running out for Roy Chapin. Returning in February 1936 from an exhausting business trip to Washington, DC, he fell ill with pneumonia. The antibiotics that would have made short work of the illness were still six or seven years in the future, and within a few days Chapin was dead. He was one week short of his fifty-sixth birthday.

Right: Convertible's doors are generously wide and open in a nearly 90-degree arc for easy entry and exit. Far right: Back seat room is somewhat cramped, however. Bottom: There's very good trunk space to be found in back.

The White Triangle

For many years the inverted white triangle (actually, a brass triangle at the very beginning) was one of motordom's most familiar trademarks, akin to the Ford signature, or the Chevrolet "bow tie," or the six-pointed star of the early Dodge.

Oddly enough, the significance of the emblem is still—after all these years—open to dispute. At least three theories have been advanced. Take your choice:

1. The three sides of the triangle represented the three principal partners involved in the establishment of Hudson as an independent company: Chapin, Coffin and Bezner.

2. The triad stood for "Performance, Service, and Value."

3. The three facets symbolized the elements of the transaction when an automobile is built and sold: the builder, the seller, the buyer.

The choice is yours. Perhaps Roy D. Chapin and his associates intended to be enigmatic about it

Denise (3-1/2), but not enough for our long legs! (The kids, by the way, love this car—especially when the top is down.) Front seat leg room is another matter entirely. It's ample. So is head room, both front and rear.

Flipping the canvas top is supposed to be handled by means of a hydraulic mechanism, but to date that part bas not been restored. Lowering it by hand is easy, however, even for one person.

We've detested idiot lights ever since we first saw them on a neighbor's new Hudson, back in 1935. On this car they are arguably the worst ever, being positioned on the glove compartment door, clear over on the right-hand side of the car. The location does great things for dashboard symmetry, but it's precious little help to the driver.

There are a few things we'd have wanted to change if this were 1946 and we were driving a new Hudson. But not very many; and probably even our short list comes mostly from the wisdom of hindsight. For the truth is, we can very easily imagine ourselves, in that exciting postwar time, selecting this fine car for our own, as the fulfillment of the dream that all of us—GIs especially—had been nurturing throughout the long, wartime years. It's a beauty; it's distinctive; it's well engineered. And it's built to last ◑

Acknowledgments and Bibliography Automotive and Aviation Industries, *October 1, 1945, March 15, 1946;* Mechanix Illustrated, *June 1946;* Motor, *October 1945, May 1946;* Motor's Handbook, *25th edition:* National Cyclopedia of American Biography; *Maurice D. Hendry,* "Hudson," Automobile Quarterly, *Vol. IX, No. 4; John Conde,* The Cars That Hudson Built; *Jerry Heasley,* The Production Figure Book for US Cars; *Richard M. Langworth,* Encyclopedia of American Cars, 1940-1970; *James H. Maloney and George H. Dammann,* Encyclopedia of American Cars, 1946-1959.

Our thanks to Melvin "Red" Burke, Fort Bragg, California; Ralph Dunwoodie, Sun Valley, Nevada; D.J. Kava, Beaumont, Texas; Mike Lamm, Stockton, California. Special thanks to Tom and Lynn Burke, Concord, California.

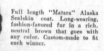

57

By Michael Lamm, Editor

12,000 Miles Later

SIA's Hudson staff car almost halves Mercedes' per-mile cost despite shameful gas mileage.

S IA's BERZOOKY EDITORS intend to find out—can a 1952 Hudson Hornet on Medicare serve as this magazine's day-in, day-out workhorse?" We asked that question back in June 1972 [see Low-Bucks Staff Car, *SIA* #11]. Now, 18 months later, we have an answer.

The answer is yes, it can, but no, the car and the experiment didn't really come up to all expectations. I had hoped for more reliability and better economy. The Hornet's shop down-time and repair costs were higher than expected (a total of about six weeks down and $360.63 cash outlay), and fuel mileage—at 10.3 mpg—almost put me in the hospital.

Yet despite these disappointments, the dowager Hornet still lives and breathes fire, and it did beat the national average for cost-per-mile economy. All considered, it's still cheaper to drive a car like this than most newer ones. I imagine that if you were to pick a collectible car that gave better gas mileage and needed fewer repairs, you could get cost-per-mile down below a Volkswagen's.

The typical American driver, so the AAA tells us, spends $1,647 a year to support his automotive habit. That's for fuel, depreciation, insurance, maintenance, license, taxes, and the rest. This averages out to 16.5¢ a mile, based on 10,000 miles of annual driving. Keep the AAA figure in mind: 16.5¢ a mile. It's official (" ") and a good theoretical yardstick, but remember, too, that in actual practice a car's cost per mile varies according to its size, popularity, your driving habits, and where you live.

I drive, as you know, the '52 Hollywood coupe you see pictured here, and I live in Stockton, California. Long-time *SIA* readers will recall that I bought this car in June 1971 from an 81-year-old Stocktonian. The odometer showed just under

76,000 miles at that time. I paid $350 for the car, and it was in good, good condition.

I've always had a soft spot for Hudsons, because my dad drove them from 1939 through the bitter end in 1954. Besides bringing back all those fond childhood memories, I consider Hudsons extremely well built and over-engineered. That opinion hasn't changed—I'm still prejudiced in favor of Hudsons.

Before putting the Hornet on the road back in 1971, I spent another $934.82 by way of refurbishments. I use the word refurbishments because this wasn't a restoration. The Hornet is very presentable, but it's never been in anything near show condition, nor was the idea to turn it into a prize winner. My plan has always been to make this car a guinea pig—an experiment to see if a 20-year-old (now 22-) car can survive everyday driving with reliability and economy. It had to do that, I felt, without any coddling.

My initial reasoning went like this: Since a Hudson can't depreciate, and since it's likely to appreciate as time passes, it and many cars like it should logically make sound, economical transportation. The question, then, is, are such cars reliable, dependable, comfortable, and usable on an everyday basis? I'd like to explore my own log book and conclusions. You can then make up your mind.

A Basis For Comparison

ROAD & TRACK Magazine publishes a series of Extended Use Reports, and these have always interested me a great deal, especially since I participate in a similar series for POPULAR MECHANICS called Owners Reports. Both involve living with a car for a long period of time. Most magazine road tests, including *SIA*'s driveReports, take only a day or so for the editors to complete, so they're all

Originally published in Special Interest Autos #21, Mar.-Apr. 1974

tors to complete, so they're all right for quick impressions, but they never reveal all of a car's quirks—not the things a real car owner uncovers after a year or two behind the wheel.

I felt it appropriate, then, to use one of *R&T*'s Extended Use Reports as the model for my own experiences with the Hornet. I picked as my basis of comparison the car that *R&T* editor Ron Wakefield owned for 24,000 miles, a 1973 Mercedes-Benz 280 4-door sedan. Laugh not!

There's a difference, true, between driving up to someone's front door in a new Mercedes and doing the same in a 22-year-old Hudson. Even so, they're more alike than not. First and least important, both use in-line 6s and unit bodies. Second, they weigh nearly the same—the Hornet is only 250 pounds heavier despite being considerably bigger in every external dimension. Third, Mercedes and Hudson share similar long-standing reputations for quality, handling, performance, driving comfort, and as long-distance road cars. Fourth, in their day, both left indelible marks in racing (though not the Mercedes 280).

Their greatest difference comes in price, the upshot being that the Mercedes cost 22.2¢ a mile to drive and the Hudson cost 11.6¢ a mile. The Hornet, then, fell sweetly below the national AAA average, but in fairness, it didn't do so well as *R&T*'s Opel Manta, which averaged 10.6¢ a mile over a 12,000-mile Extended Use Report. Let's continue with our Mercedes/Hudson comparison by category.

Horrible Gas Mileage

The Mercedes averaged 16.4 mpg for *R&T*'s 24,000 miles of driving. That's quite a bit better than the Hornet's shocking 10.3 mpg. Yes, 10.3 mpg stinks, but the figure is accurate, unfortunately, and if it's any consolation, it came with regular-grade fuel, most of it around 30¢ a gallon at the time.

When mechanic Jim Holmes and I overhauled the Hornet's engine three winters ago, I swapped the stock manifold and 2-barrel carburetor for Hudson's Twin-H-Power setup. More glamour, I figured, and maybe even some better acceleration and gas mileage. The Twin-H manifold came from a local wrecking yard, but the Twin-H Carter W-l carbs were new-old stock, still in their boxes. I bought them by mail from a fellow in New York, knowing full well that they were meant for the 1954 Twin-H, not the '52. In 1952, Twin-H upped Hornet horsepower from 145 to 160 bhp gross. By 1954, standard Hornets were pulling a base 160 bhp without Twin-H, and the dual carbs supposedly added another 10 bhp.

Now, whether having the wrong W-l carbs reduces gas mileage or whether it would be that low anyway I don't know. I do know that MOTOR TREND, in their test of a 1953 Twin-H Hornet, averaged 13.3 mpg in city driving, and ROAD & TRACK averaged 9.5 mpg for their 1952 Hornet! That's already bad, especially for factory-tuned test cars, but then when I consider that I did drive on the freeway at 70-80 mph (this was before the present 55-mph limit, which I now observe religiously), and that I make lots of quick trips in town, I believe the l0.3-mpg figure stands to reason.

I realize that my Hudson-driving friends will gnash their teeth at the 10.3-mpg admission. Sure, a Twin-H Hornet can do better. Feather-feet might get 16-17 mpg. If you calculate mileage on only one tank of gas, you can get any figure you want. My calculations span 12,000 miles of every type of driving, though, some of it fast, some pokey, so this check is definitely accurate.

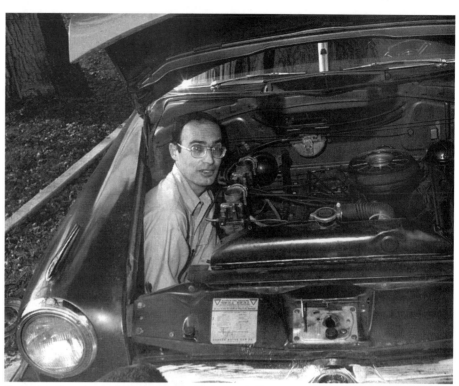

Happy the editor who can find a Saturday to play. Among the Hornet's blessings is plenty of underhood workspace. Fender panel unbolts, lifts out in 10 minutes, gives fine access to tappets.

Hornet convertible parts car lives behind garage, recently donated its rear axle for a transplant.

Comparing Pocketbooks—SIA's Hornet vs. R&T's Mercedes	1973 Mercedes-Benz 280, 2 years & 24,000 mi.	1952 Hudson Hornet 1 year & 12,000 mi.
Initial price	$ 9,377.00	$ 350.00
Refurbishing expenses	----	934.82
Repairs & replacements	268.00	360.63
Routine maintenance	230.00	39.98
Gasoline	600.00 (2 yrs.)	771.10 (1 yr.)
License & taxes	306.00 (2 yrs.)	32.00 (1 yr.)
Insurance (see below)	548.00 (2 yrs.)	122.82 (1 yr.)
Total expenses	**$11,329.00**	**$ 2,611.35**
Resale value (est.)	6,000.00	1,250.00
Cost of driving	5,329.00 (2 yrs.)	1,395.71 (1 yr.)
Overall av. cost per mile	**22.2¢**	**11.6¢**

Note: Mercedes-Benz figures courtesy *Road & Track* Magazine, Oct. 1973. Insurance on the Mercedes was 15/30/10 with $100 deductible collision & uninsured motorist. Insurance on the Hudson was (is) 25/50/10 with no collision and 15/30 uninsured

Hornet shines in roadability, handling, and as long-distance mover. As a road car it rivals Mercedes. Fatigued axle (right) snapped at 85,695 miles.

Whether it's typical I don't know. I suspect it is. Different jets or metering rods might help.

When I get a chance, too, I want to re-install the old 2-barrel stock manifold and run another 12,000-mile check. We'll see.

Routine Maintenance—How Much?

I change oil every 1,000 miles and hand-lube the Hornet myself at 2,000-mile intervals. Oil by the case costs 39¢ a quart (Standard 30-W detergent), as opposed to 80¢ at the station. Chassis grease costs 29¢ a tube, enough for a dozen lubes. I own a pair of J.C. Whitney steel lift ramps ($14 five years ago) and a cheap creeper ($9.95), which I figure have paid for themselves by now.

I installed an AC oil filter after we overhauled the engine. I change filter elements every 5,000 miles. The Hornet burns no oil between changes, but it does drool a little from the rear main seal. *R&T*'s Mercedes also had a leaky main seal, but this was fixed under warranty. The Hudson, being slightly off warranty, continues to leak, because dropping the pan makes replacement a complicated repair.

In summary, the Mercedes' routine maintenance was $115 a year. The Hudson's, $39.98.

How About Repairs?

Repairs are another story. You'll remember that I'd nursed the old 4-speed Hydra-Matic along for several thousand miles in 1972 by changing fluid and adjusting the throttle rod for smoother shifts. I managed to sidestep an overhaul for a while, but eventually the 2-3 shift got rough again, and at 80,660 miles, this roughness forced me to the transmission shop. It was tearing the devil out of U-joints and the rear axle, causing all sorts of play in the drivetrain and, as I would find out 5,000 miles later, this play had already weakened the right rear axle shaft so badly that it would eventually snap.

I took the car to the only good transmission shop here in town, and for $211.68 they put the Hydro back to rights. Or at least partially back, because I had to return twice more to let them correct a sticky shift from forward to reverse and also a hesitation going into fourth under load. In all, transmission repairs accounted for about 10 days of downtime, including one weekend.

308-cid L-head 6 with optional 2-carb setup and Hydra-Matic averaged only 10.3 mpg in 12,000 miles. Performance is adequate but not startling. Everything would improve with overdrive.

Major Repairs in 11,590 Miles

Date	Mileage	Repair	Cost
6/19/72	77,594	Clean & resolder radiator	$26.50
9/13/72	78,901	Muffler, replace	19.37
11/7/72	80,660	Overhaul Hydra-Matic	211.68
12/14/72	80,695	Center driveline bushing	6.00*
1/4/73	81,230	Balance one front tire	2.00
1/4/73	81,230	Set up brakes	3.00
2/1/73	82,612	2 steering bearings	6.87*
9/1/73	85,502	Gasket set & valves	14.75*
9/4/73	85,502	Valve job, labor	10.00
9/12/73	85,695	2 bushings for axle	5.21
9/12/73	85,695	Machinework on bushings	12.50
9/12/73	85,695	Install new 3rd member, labor	42.75
		Total	**$360.63**

* Asterisk denotes no labor or installation charge.

specifications

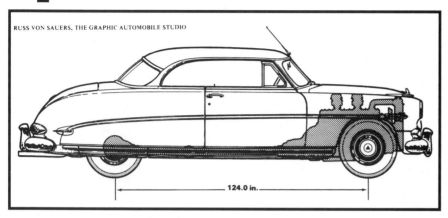

RUSS VON SAUERS, THE GRAPHIC AUTOMOBILE STUDIO

124.0 in.

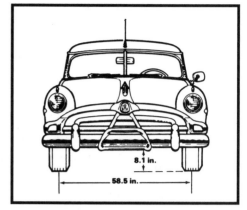

8.1 in.
58.5 in.

1952 Hudson Hornet 7B Hollywood hardtop coupe

Price when new	$2,790 f.o.b. Detroit (1952)
Options	Radio, heater, Hydra-Matic, Twin-H-Power, day/night mirror.

ENGINE

Type	In-line L-head 6, water-cooled, cast-iron block, 4 mains, full-pressure lubrication
Bore x stroke	3.8125 inches x 4.5 inches
Displacement	308 cubic inches
Max. bhp @ rpm	160 @ 3,800
Max. torque @ rpm	260 @ 1,800
Compression ratio	7.2:1
Induction system	Twin 1-bbl. carbs, mechanical fuel pump.
Exhaust system	Cast-iron manifold, single muffler and resonator.
Electrical system	6-volt battery/coil

TRANSMISSION

Type	Hydra-Matic, 4-speed automatic, torque converter, planetary gears.
Ratios: 1st	3.82:1
2nd	2.63:1
3rd	1.45:1
4th	1.00:1
Reverse	4.30:1

CLUTCH

Type	None

DIFFERENTIAL

Type	Hypoid, Hotchkiss drive.
Ratio	3.07:1
Drive axles	Semi-floating

STEERING

Type	Worm & roller
Turns lock-to-lock	5.75
Ratio	20.4:1
Turn circle	42 ft.

BRAKES

Type	4-wheel hydraulic drums, internal expanding, with mechanical reserve.
Drum diameter	11.0 inches.
Total lining area	158.7 square inches.

CHASSIS & BODY

Frame	Unitized with body, perimeter type with bolt-on front subframe.
Body construction	All steel, welded.
Body style	2-dr., 6-pass. hardtop coupe.

SUSPENSION

Front	Independent unequal A-arms, coil springs, tubular hydraulic shock absorbers.
Rear	Longitudinal leaf springs, tubular hydraulic shock absorbers, anti-roll bar.
Tires	7.60 x 15 tube type whitewalls.
Wheels	Pressed steel discs, drop-center rims, lug-bolted to brake drums.

WEIGHTS AND MEASURES

Wheelbase	124.0 inches
Overall length	208.0 inches
Overall width	77.6 inches
Overall height	60.4 inches
Front tread	58.5 inches
Rear tread	55.5 inches
Ground clearance	8.1 inches
Curb weight	3,660 lb.

CAPACITIES

Crankcase	7 qt.
Cooling system	19.5 qt.
Fuel tank	20 gal.

FUEL CONSUMPTION

Best	14.0 mpg.
Average	10.3 mpg.

PERFORMANCE (from **Motor Trend,** 8/52 test of 145-bhp Hornet sedan):

0-30 mph	5.2 sec.
0-40 mph	7.8 sec.
0-50 mph	11.3 sec.
0-60 mph	16.8 sec.
0-70 mph	20.1 sec.
Standing 1/4-mile	20.2 sec and 70.2 mph.
Top speed (av.)	99.2 mph.

I blame the transmission's pre-overhaul roughness for causing the right rear axle to snap 5,000 miles later. Ironically, the *R&T* Mercedes similarly needed a right rear axle replacement. It didn't snap, but some lock washers omitted at the factory let it slip out of its wheel. Mercedes again fixed *R&T*'s axle under warranty, but in the Hornet's case, I had to pirate another axle from my single remaining parts car. I took out the entire axle assembly from the parts cars, removed the axle shafts and third member, and used these in the Hollywood. The rest of the parts-car differential became a potters wheel for the kids.

You might wonder how the Hornet axle actually snapped. I was driving about 25 mph along a 2-lane city street and wanted to pass another car. When I kicked down from fourth to third, the engine revved freely. There was absolutely no connection between the engine and the rear wheels. I thought at first a spline had let go. I've heard since that snapped axles in Hornets aren't too uncommon and that for racing, Hudson used shafts as thick as your wrist.

The third major breakdown in 12,000 miles took

place on a trip back from L.A. last fall. Driving north on U.S. 99 at about 75 mph, I suddenly felt the car slow down. I thought at first that I'd hit a strong headwind. I didn't think much about it and simply pushed harder on the gas. Next thing I noticed was the temperature gauge creeping up toward H, so I backed off to 55 mph. The temp needle held steady at that speed, but whenever I'd try to go faster, the engine would start to heat.

I drove along that way for about 60 miles, when I had to stop for gas. Idling at the first light off the freeway, I felt the car shake as if the engine were missing on one cylinder. It was. I hoped it was a bad plug, but a quick check at the filling station showed me it wasn't. I nursed the car home at 50 mph (this was long before the gasoline crunch). At home, a compression check confirmed what had happened. That first "headwind" was a slowing down due to one valve no longer sealing. Why did it burn? Probably because after Jim and I overhauled the engine, we adjusted the valves cold but never reset them hot. Lesson learned, and that surely wasn't any fault of the Hudson's.

Jim Holmes performed the valve job. He replaced not one but three bad valves. The valve job cost me very little ($24.75), but with waiting for valves, gaskets, and then with some bad luck toward the buttoning-up process, the Hornet was out of commission for no less than six weeks. That's a hazard of owning an obsolete make. Luckily I had a backup car—my Camaro—so I wasn't in a hurry to have the Hudson back.

You understand, of course, that this repair and most of the others weren't performed in commercial shops. If they had been, the cost would have been greater but the down time might have been less (although not necessarily). The Hornet's other, less major,<None> repairs are listed in the chart on the facing page.

Driving Around Town

People tend to smile when they see the Hornet. It gives them a little lift, I suppose, which in turn gives me a little lift. Many are curious to inspect it, and one of the car's hazards is its stigma as an attractive nuisance. Other drivers crane to see it. I've had quite a few people stop me as I'm driving down the street.

One fellow in a red Chevy pickup cut a U-turn in the middle of Miner Avenue to catch up with the Hudson. He motioned me to stop. I did, and I knew what he was going to ask. "Want to sell it? Is it for sale?" I said no, but we stood there and talked for 15 minutes about Hudsons.

Lots of people want to buy the car. They'll zoom up behind me on the freeway, heave alongside, and I can read the driver's lips. "Wanna sell it?" I shake my head no, we wave, and off he goes again.

Sometimes on the freeway, people will want to play games. Kids, especially. They'll pass and then sit in front of me, watching their mirrors. I'll pass them once, and if they pass me again after that, I slow way down. Eventually they get bored and go away.

On the other hand, it's a fantastic filling station car. Attendants leap to it. It's hard to beat for making friends fast. If ever I need a favor at a gas station—directions, a road map, to use the phone, john, or lube rack—no problem. It's a great conversation starter with just about everybody. People loosen up. I've watched little old ladies walk all the way around the car. People tell me about the time they or their uncles or their neighbors owned Hudsons. "Now there was a fantastic car."

How Is It On Long Trips?

When *SIA* began this experiment back in mid-1972, I figured we (the staff) would put about 15,000 miles a year on the car. It hasn't worked out that way. I'm now the only staffer who drives it, and it took me 18 months to put on these 12,000 miles. Just over half that mileage came in short, in-town trips. The other half involved longer hauls: five runs back and forth to Los Angeles, each averaging 1,000 miles; two to Reno (500 miles each); and an unrecorded number to San Francisco, Oakland, and the Bay Area. I use the car for pleasure as well as business, and occasionally my wife and I have taken friends in it to restaurants and social affairs. Mostly, though, it's a business car.

It's on the freeway at sustained high speeds of 70-80 mph that the Hornet feels really at home. All Stepdown Hudsons share a reputation as long-distance runners. This car's effortless long-range cruising and its great comfort are the best things about it. I can spend 5-1/2 hours behind

Super-wide armrest separates kids, can serve as writing table. Check thin pillars, ample head room.

the wheel on a hot summer day and still step out refreshed, even without air conditioning. Seating position, wheel height, good ventilation, and the gentle but firm ride all contribute.

Going to Reno, U.S. 80 over the Sierra crosses Donner Summit at 7,227 feet. I've driven this route many times in other cars, and all but the Hornet have pooped out near the top. Even *R&T*'s Mercedes elicited this remark, "At 8,000-ft elevation the car had lost all its zip...." But the Hornet hadn't. I don't believe the Hudson's speed has ever fallen below 65 mph on U.S. 80 over the Sierra. Same over the Grapevine going to L.A.

Handling is superb. There's neither over- nor understeer, and except for some wheel fight, fast cornering presents no problem. I've never broken the tires loose despite some very quick maneuvers in which I tried to do just that. Highway bends marked for 50 mph can be taken at 75 in comfort, with very little sway or roll. In some cars, too, fast cornering makes for driver confusion—too many different, unpredictable things coming up too quickly. Not with the Hornet. Fast turns are as easy as long straight stretches.

I do want to mention the tires. You might remember that when I first put the Hornet on the road, it had a set of 12-year-old, new-old-stock U.S. Royals—2-1/2-in. whitewalls. I didn't trust these, so I put on four new Lesters. The Lesters haven't given me a bit of trouble. They've been over the freeways in 110° heat, have never had a puncture much less a blowout, I haven't babied them a bit, and they still show absolutely no wear. Tread depth looks unaffected by 12,000 miles of pretty hard driving.

What I do miss in this car is power steering. I thought perhaps I'd install it at one time, and I looked for a Hudson parts car that had it. Never found one, probably because at $177 new, power steering wasn't a popular option. The Hornet's unassisted steering is heavy and makes tight parking a real tussle. Most women couldn't fit this car into a short spot. Most men can't. I'd still like to install power.

What's it Like Inside?

For a car on a 124-inch wheelbase, there's precious little leg room in the back seat. Plenty up front but not much in the rear. My children find the seatbacks almost too heavy to push forward, and the seats' weight tends to catapult passengers rearward when they get in. Everyone trips at first on the perimeter frame (step up and then down), even though many newer cars are also "step-

Hornet poses at Donner Pass on way to Harrah's, Reno. High elevations don't leave it puffing.

down" by now. The huge doors tend to be awkward, especially in tight parking slots. The doors don't always shut without hard slamming, but luckily they rattle if they're not closed all the way.

What I like about the interior are the many little touches-things you don't find in cars nowadays. There are *five* domelights that come on with the doors, so the interior is like surgery. The seatbacks have big map pockets plus thick robe cords. There's a wide center armrest in the rear seat—the kids love it.

Both benches are fantastically wide. People marvel at how huge the front compartment is. Hudsons were among the first cars to have front seats wider than the car was tall. The seats are also very deep and buoyant.

Most Stepdown Hudsons had windows like tank slits, with fair-sized blind spots at the rear quarters of sedans and regular coupes. Luckily, the Hollywood hardtop has vast expanses of glass and almost no pillars to cut vision. By today's standards, the roof stands awfully tall. There's half a foot of air between the top of my head and the roof.

Two things do bother me about the interior. One is glare from those great expanses of chrome on the instrument panel. It looks nice, but it's dangerous when driving east around 5:00 p.m. The other bother is that the side windows don't seal well at the top. They whistle at freeway speeds.

Great care went into building Hudsons. I've searched for glue runs, sloppy mastic, shoddy fit and finish, and I haven't found any yet. Having replaced windows and even fenders, I find that workmanship is as faultless in the Hornet's hidden areas as on the surface. I don't say that Hudson was alone in its standard of quality. I believe all American cars were more carefully put together in those days.

Depreciation & General Expense

When *SIA* announced back in June 1972 that we'd try this experiment, we valued the Hornet at $850, despite having $1,121.10 in it at that time. I now value the car at $1,250, an appreciation of $400, and I feel I could easily get that for it today. (I'm writing this on Dec. 16, 1973, and I realize that by the time you read these words, the nation's economy and old-car prices might dictate an

Editor drives this car mostly for business but also uses it for family and social functions.

Freeway cruising used to be an easy 70 mph, but no more. Chromy dash panel sometimes dazzles.

entirely different value.) By totaling initial price, repairs, replacements, and refurbishments only, I find I have $1,695.45 in the car. That means that despite appreciating $400 in one year, actual out-of-pocket loss was $445.45. We can call that depreciation, although technically it's normal expense and investment. If I don't put more into the Hornet, I can probably recoup the investment later on.

R&T's Mercedes depreciated $3,377 in 24,000 miles of driving. Depreciation was, in fact, the M-B's largest single expense. And it's the largest expense of owning any new or newer car today.

By way of summary, I feel that the Hornet has much more than a low cost-per-mile figure going for it. In the first place, the owner of a brand-new car can also expect a couple of weeks of downtime. My POPULAR MECHANICS Owners Reports confirm this. And if new-car owners had to pay for repairs (warranty doesn't cover everything), they'd likely spend as much as I did in 12,000 miles.

As for gas mileage, most full-sized 1974 cars don't do much better than 10.3 mpg. The Hornet, though, ought to.

By eliminating the Hornet's two major drains (poor mileage and high repair expenses), I say that a 20-year-old car in good condition makes an incomparably better investment than a new one. It does even with the repairs and low gas mileage. Besides, consider the intangibles—the pleasure and enjoyment of driving a car like the Hornet which, despite its age, will still be breathing fire long after this crop of cars is gone and forgotten. ☜

Our thanks to ROAD & TRACK Magazine, Box 1757, Newport Beach, California 92660; members of the Hudson-Essex-Terraplane Club, Peter Booz, Treasurer, 23104 Dolorosa, Woodland Hills, California 91364; Jim Holmes, Stockton, California; POPULAR MECHANICS, 224 W. 57th St. New York, NY 10019; and Jack Clifford, Clifford Research & Development Corp., Costa Mesa. California.

The Hudson Hornet, to many enthusiasts and students of automotive design, was the high-water mark of the independent manufacturers' design studios. Perhaps there is a valid argument in favor of the Raymond Lowey-designed Studebaker Starliner, but few post-war cars made or left as great an impression as the Hornet. Whether in convertible form, traditional "family"-style four-door or, in the case of this truly fine specimen, a two-door Club Coupe, the Hornet had no equal when it first appeared in 1951. It was the pinnacle of a design evolution that surprisingly began just before World War II.

In 1941, Hudson built a single prototype designed by Hudson's forward-thinking designer, Frank Spring. It was sleek and of unit-body construction, which allowed the car a much lower profile than was currently fashionable. It was like nothing seen before. It was this lower profile that proved the car's undoing. Hudson President A. E. Barit saw it and complained that it was "too low" for what he felt the public favored. The sleek design study would sit dormant until after World War II, when the direc-

The chrome alloy in-line six block is fed via a pair of Carter type WGD 2-barrel carbs with distinctive red air cleaner boxes on each.

tion of automotive design was wide open to creativity. It must be remembered that in 1948 most cars being sold were pretty much nothing more than slightly updated pre-war models. So huge was the demand for new cars that it mattered little that there were no innovations or fresh designs for the first few immediate years after the cessation of hostilities.

Aviation, during the war, had gripped the public's attention and imagination, and attempts were made to incorporate these aircraft themes into auto design. Streamlined body styles were the precursors to the often-garish fins and other aircraft accoutrements that would be hung on cars over the next decade or so. Frank Spring realized that the time was right, made a few changes to his "pre-war" design study and gave it to Barit again. This time however, after spending some quality time behind the wheel, Mr. Barit was impressed enough with the car's road manner to sign it into production for 1948. At 60 inches high, it was the lowest-profile car offered that year. This design was offered as the Super Six, the Commodore Six, and the top-of-the-line Commodore Eight.

The Hornet first appeared in 1951, and featured a new L-head, 308-cu.in. straight-six engine that churned out a respectable 145 hp. Although a Six, it turned out roughly 30 percent more torque than the previous Hudson straight-eight. This reverting to a six-cylinder engine would later prove to seriously limit Hudson's success in the mid-fifties. Clearly, the industry was moving towards the V-8 engine, and Hudson would never recover in time to thwart its own demise.

In 1951, Hudson took a step that many bigger manufacturers had already

Stinging Sensation

Cruising Tucson in a 1953 Hudson Hornet Club Coupe

By Don Spiro
Photography by the author

taken. They began a factory effort in NASCAR Grand National racing that would prove successful over the next three years. It gave Hudson much "free" publicity to a car-buying public that was fast becoming enamored with speed and performance. "Win on Sunday, sell on Monday," which was to be the credo of the Big Three for the ensuing decades, was realized early on by a small independent. Notable Hornet pilots in NASCAR were Marshall Teague, Herb Thomas, and Lee Petty. In spite of many racing successes, Hudson, like other independent makers, offered too little, too late to an increasingly savvy

buying public. They clearly lacked the capital to get a new model to market in the short time afforded the cash-heavy deep pockets of the Big Three.

The ultimate causes of the demise of the Hudson marque have been well documented (see *SIA* #134). Poor planning, a lack of a timely V-8, and the belated introduction of a small lightweight model, along with the undoing of other independent manufacturers, led to their merger with Nash, and the final death knell for this most beloved carmaker. Happily though there are still fine examples of Hornets to be savored. This 1953 Hornet Club Coupe, owned by Ron

Sotardi of Tucson, Arizona, is as fine an example as you're ever likely to find.

Ron has owned this Hornet since 1991. It is one of four cars in his collection, the others being a '50 Cadillac, a '31 Ford Model A Deluxe two-door, and a repro Cord convertible that he drives more often than the other three. Ron says, "That's just a fun car to run to local shows with the top down." The Hudson is the only one in his collection that Ron hasn't restored himself. "The car came from Virginia, and was bought by someone who thought they could do a show-quality ground-up restoration on a budget," Ron told us. "When this fellow finally realized he couldn't do the impossible, he sold it to another owner who thought he could do the same thing: me! Well, I fast found out that I couldn't, and had the car restored at a shop on Long Island.

"To me, the 1953 Hornet is the zenith of Hornet development. The experience of racing in '51 and '52 much improved the '53 Hornet, most notably in the beefed-up rear axle and suspension. It improved greatly the car's handling, which accounted for its racing success. I find the handling and road manner-isms of the Hornet to be its finest fea-tures. Considering it still rolls on origi-nal-spec, bias-ply tires, there are few cars from that period that handle as well as the Hornet. The same goes for the brakes: The dual-circuit system gives much finer control of braking than any other car I own, including the Cadillac. Style-wise you cannot beat the seductive 'Bustle Back Look,' a refer-ence to infamous past women's fashion. I never tire of staring at the swoop and curves of the Hornet's rear end. It just looks great!

"Of course the car has its downside as well. It has a voracious appetite for gas for a six-cylinder. The 'Twin H Power' carburetor set-up, while a fine per-former, drinks gas to the tune of 16 miles per gallon. My '50 Cadillac, in contrast, is heavier but delivers 19 or 20 miles per gallon on the highway. There are design and engineering features, or lack of features, which are a nuisance when performing maintenance. For ex-ample, to adjust the valve sleeves you have to remove the inner fender liners on the Hornet. This is a cumbersome task for the home mechanic, as many components have to be removed before the liners can come off. This is a simple task on other cars from that period. Same goes for working on the rear sus-pension. To gain access, you have to disassemble most of the rear interior to get to the fenderwells. I also find rear visibility poor. Driver-side rear-view mirrors were, incredibly when you think of it today, a dealer-installed option on the Hornet! These shortcomings are far outweighed, though, by the fine design and driveability of the coupe, however. I just love this car!"

Personally, I have always liked the sleek design of the Hornet. While pho-tographing Ron's car for Hemmings' "2001 Cars of the Fifties calendar," I was able to study and appreciate the subtle nuances of Spring's step-down design, as Tucson provided a spectacular sun-set that danced off the curvaceous flanks of the Hornet. There really aren't any bad lines on the car; it borders on sexy from many angles, and the design has aged gracefully over close to half a century of time. Not surprisingly, on some levels, it still works, in this day

Minimal front body overhang contributed to its fine handling.

Aircraft-inspired hood ornament was very pop-ular in the Fifties.

Lavish dashboard covered in acres of chrome.

and age of bulbous—or, as a good friend states, "the melted-dish-of-ice-cream"—design rampant in the industry. When Ron offered his Hornet for a test drive, I was thrilled and, at the same time, a bit anxious heading out into the late after-noon Tucson traffic with such a pristine classic. It was to be the very character-istics that earned Mr. Barit's approval in 1948, and make the car so appealing to Ron today, that I found astonishing in a car almost 50 years old.

As I settled into the Hornet's sofa-like seat and wrapped my hands around the steering wheel, my entire collective sense of automotive "scale" disappeared. This cabin was vast in comparison to those of the cars I had been using since I passed my driving test back in 1969. My automotive experience since that tri-umphant day has been gleaned primar-ily behind the wheel of a succession of Nordic Volvos and SAABS. Modest in size, fine handling (well, in the case of the SAABs), and long on safety features, my interiors were snug and intimate. They were a blend of tastefully colored cloth with all dash surfaces and con-trols finished in a no-nonsense, pur-poseful and yielding black plastic. This Hudson's dashboard, though, was like none I'd ever seen, even in similar-era cars from other manufacturers. The enormous dashboard stretching out in front of me clearly was from another age. It was as if the entire massive dash-

board had been hewn from a single resisting mass of glowing steel ingot. Its mass and strength were impressive and in-your-face. And the chrome finish! This was not merely chrome as a deco-rative element; this dashboard was *Chromed Steel Squared.* I have never stared at a dashboard and seen such a multitude of my quizzical and distorted faces staring back at me from every sur-face. I felt like I was in a fun-house hall of mirrors. From the tasteful deco-like faceplates and gauge nacelles, to every control, stalk, knob, instrument, cli-mate control, horn ring, and radio all shimmered triple chrome in the after-noon light. Even the steering column was encased in a gleaming chrome sleeve!

I have not gripped a steering wheel as smooth and as large in diameter, and at the same time as thin and delicate as this one. My hands were accustomed over the years to thick Nardi or similar small-diameter, leather-wrapped after-market steering wheels. As I would later learn, there was a simple reason for the large wheel, based on the laws of physics: Steering a car this size necessi-tated the big wheel. Remember, not everyone driving back then was "pumped" after a stint in the service. Housewives and mothers in post-war America were being redefined as "deli-cate homebodies," after half a decade of the no-nonsense, "We Can Do It," Rosie

Hornet's happy owner, Ron Sotardi, proclaims, "I just love this car!"

Windshield visor very effective, but causes drag.

the Riveter image. And June Cleaver was just lurking around the next bend to further stifle the once strong feminine image. A big wheel gave ample leverage for the more delicate women drivers. "Room for six" was an understatement, even in this two-door configuration. Neither Ron nor I qualify as petite, and yet there was ample room for a third adult on the supple bench between us. As for the back seat, three adults or five or so wide-eyed, screaming baby boomers, heading out for ice cream on a sultry summer evening, could ride easily. This was a cabin built expressly for a rapidly expanding post-war family and long comfortable drives to nowhere in particular on weekends. In the words of David Byrne and the Talking Heads, I had indeed found myself "behind the wheel of a large automobile...."

I am always eager to drive a car that is almost my age. The L-head six fired and turned over with a turn of the dash-mounted key. To the foot, the engine seemed smooth and respectably responsive for a post-war straight-six. Slipping the long chromed column lever into low, I gingerly rolled the Hornet off the shoulder onto the two-lane road. Ron sensed my wariness of the car's size at once and exclaimed, "You can get on it if you like." Those words caused a bit of embarrassment but, thankfully, inspired a higher degree of confidence. The Hudson, while no rocket, accelerated smoothly, with authority, and exhibited no body shake or rattles whatsoev-

er. The car seemed solid and surefooted on the road, and wandered little on straight pavement. Very little course "correction" was necessary, something I always seem to be aware of in early fifties cars. Ahead of us, the road, while straight, undulated severely as it crossed a series of dry desert washes. I slowed somewhat, but after the first quick rise and fall I began to see why this suspension garnered the stock-car reputation for fine handling in its time. I fully expected a car this size to wallow and bottom out on each wash, but was surprised at its resiliency and ability to collect itself so quickly. Compared to other driving experiences of similar-era cars, especially those from the Big Three, the Hornet indeed seemed "Head of the Class" in handling. The period ads, it seems, were true and the impressive NASCAR record was deserved.

When the road broadened into four lanes and the traffic thinned out, Ron recommended I give it the "swerve" test around some imaginary pylons on the road. While certainly not an autocross or road-racing candidate, the Hudson responded in a manner for which I was totally unprepared. While the skinny two-ply tires let me know it was not something they would tolerate for long, not once did the Hudson seem overly tail heavy or get way out of sorts as the weight transferred side to side. Steering input required soft hands, but the car's response was surprising. It was fun to watch the wing-like sun visor begin to act like agitated flaps on an A-300 Airbus landing as speed crept over the sixty mark. The Hudson instilled a high degree of confidence, with very little time behind the wheel.

Being from the school of four-wheel disc brakes, I naturally assumed the Hornet would feel under-braked, even with a firm foot on the brake pedal. Was I mildly surprised. Braking, in no small part to the Hornet's well engineered and race-proven brake system, was sure and straight. Pedal effort was half that of what I experienced driving a '52 Buick

two weeks previously. In fact, the brakes on the Hornet seemed better than the four-wheel-drum systems on a number of cars fifteen years younger. I found the dash layout both informative and well thought out for its time. Remember, it was usually form over function, or in the case of, say, a Nash from the same period, a Spartan dash at best. Independents, like Nash, spent all their money on the outside of the car, and left little to lavish on a fancy dashboard. In the Hornet, the dash design was given as much attention as the exterior. Big, easy-to-read gauges told all vital functions at a glance, once I had oriented myself back in time. Rearward vision, however, something that should not have been a problem with the generous amount of glass and thin roof pillars, was surprisingly inadequate. Ron was correct in his assessment, "Clearly, something as simple as larger mirrors, particularly the outside one, would have corrected that shortcoming." America, in '51, was looking eagerly and optimistically forward to a bright future free of war and depression. Perhaps those small mirrors reflected a reluctance to look back too long on the two previous and trying decades. The bench seat seemed comfortable for the all-too-short time I spent behind the wheel. How one's lower back might feel after a five-hour stint is left to those who experienced the Hornet firsthand. How about lateral support in the seat when cornering? Say...what's that? I found another use for the big steering wheel as I entered a turn a little heavy on the throttle; it offers lots of surface to hang onto.

In the fading light of another perfect Tucson sunset, and much too soon, I found myself turning the Hornet into Ron's driveway. I sat for a moment and listened to the sound of fifties technology idling beyond the firewall. I had been taken back by the aesthetics and spirit of Spring's design long before I had the chance to drive one. Now that I had spent quality time behind the wheel, clearly the '53 Hornet was and is a driving experience no other car I have driven from that period can match. A set of fine radials, as wide as the wheelwells will allow, would be a change I would like to experience on a car as surprisingly driveable and well mannered as this '53 Club Coupe.

Hudson, in so many ways, was years ahead of its time in 1948. One marvels at, and at the same time is saddened by, their inability to maintain that leading position for less than a decade. Such was the state of the industry in those heady post-war years. All it took for success was money and prudent planning, something the Big Three always had in spades and something, unfortunately, the independent manufacturers like Hudson never had enough of. ❧

HUDSON JET

by Ken Gross, *Feature Editor*

There was nothing wrong with this early compact…

except that it killed the company.

Originally published in Special Interest Autos #60, Nov.-Dec. 1980

Photos by Jon Barber

Frank Spring's original design concept for the Jet was inspired by his dramatic Italia. Hudson top management, however, wanted the car to resemble a '52 Ford, and their views prevailed.

THE JET KILLED Hudson—make no mistake—but not because the model itself was a complete failure. It was simply the wrong car, at the wrong time, in the wrong country. The Jet saddled Hudson management with a $16 million development bill that didn't have a chance of seeing black ink when spread over a paltry 35,000 units.

Foreign car experts thought they had Hudson's new introduction pegged perfectly. *Road & Track*'s John Bond wrote that his first approach to the new Jet was "...mild interest—perhaps even condescension." But, at the end of his road test, Bond was a believer. "Here is a scrappy little car that is going to give the Big Three and the little three (Henry J, Rambler, and Willys) some real competition."

Across the Atlantic, the seasoned *Autocar* editors came to the same conclusion. They termed the Jet "...a car with European character," and praised its firm ride, roadholding, and braking. However, John Bond recalled for *Special Interest Autos* that the Jet's suspension was pretty mushy. "...It rolled. How it rolled. Like a sailboat without a keel. But it did stick pretty well in spite of this roll." Perhaps the *Autocar* Jet had

beefed-up export suspension?

So what went wrong? Why didn't a car-hungry American public snap up this seemingly sensibly designed, performance-oriented compact?

For starters, if looks could kill, Hudson's Jet was dead on arrival. Too, the years of voracious demand for cars, any cars, were peaking. The postwar car vacuum was nearly filled when the Jet bowed, forcing Hudson's light car to compete on even terms with the Big Three—hell, anyone could've predicted the outcome.

The annals of automotive history are filled with tales of manufacturers who thought, when times were tough, that a low-priced entry would somehow see them through. And for all the failures, the relative successes of Studebaker's Champion and Packard's 110 (see *Special Interest Autos* #35 and #11) remained shining examples for struggling independents.

Hudson management was no exception. The company's splash-oiled Essex (*Special Interest Autos* #35) gave Ford and Chevrolet a bad time the year the stock market tumbled—and the company weathered the Depression with the help of the moderately successful Terra-

plane in 1932. Clearly, with his once dramatic step-down series becoming older looking, out of style, overweight and dated, Hudson president, A.E. Barit, looked to past precedents to turn his company around.

Besides, there were stirrings of interest in small cars. The lesson was that you had to look carefully between the lines. The Henry J sold just under 82,000 units in its first 18 months but slipped to 23,568 units in its second year. Over in Kenosha, the Rambler accounted for over 50,000 units in 1951 and in 1952. But there again, the market seemed to be softening and there was still virtually no demand for European small sedans.

Independent dealers competed fiercely for their small market shares. Kaiser-Frazer and Nash dealers had a demonstrable showroom advantage— or so it must have seemed to Hudson's beleaguered sales force.

Certainly in 1951, when the Jet plans were taking shape, a reasonable market survey might have shown that the American public wasn't really ready for compact cars—not just yet, when buyers were about to take a roller coaster ride of excess—big V-8s, tailfins, longer,

HUDSON JET

lower, you know the rest. Nevertheless, automobiles are planned two to three years in advance, and Hudson management thought they'd recognized the trend that would save the business.

Dick Langworth interviewed Roy D. Chapin—Chapin was Hudson's regional sales manager In 1952. Recalling the Jet, Chapin commented, "...the thing that really caused the downfall, if you want to call it that, or accelerated it, at least, was the Jet. This should have been a successful small automobile. The dealers were just crying for a car of that type.

"We were promoting it with a drawing—that was all we had. In the drawing (remember the exaggerated illustrations of the fifties?), it wasn't a bad looking car. Unfortunately, the finished product didn't look like the drawing. It was high

and narrow and bulged in the wrong places. It's a shame because conceptually the car was excellent. I think by the time they got through making all the compromises, many of which I'm sure were necessary, it lost practically everything it started out to be and wound up a product relatively costly to build in relation to the price you probably should get for it."

Before talking about the Jet's styling, it's important to set the scene historically. The Hudson Jet was the only all-new car of 1953 and should have received maximum attention. Sadly, the boxy little car with its high roofline, narrow stance, and heavy trim looked like a shrunken Ford—and listed for nearly $200 more. (For an actual base price four-door sedan comparison, the Jet was $1,858 vs. Chevrolet $1,670, Ford $1,690, and Plymouth $1,750.)

Hudson's step-down styling had been revolutionary in 1948 and had weathered the years with detail and trim

changes. The company had precious little money available for new tooling, so subtle facelifts and changes were designed to give a "new" appearance while major sheet metal remained static.

Hindsight says Hudson would have been well advised to retool for its bread-and-butter Hornet and Wasp series, and despite the stock car-proven performance from the big Twin Power sixes, develop its own V-8 to follow the emerging fashion.

When the decision was made, probably in late 1950 or early 1951, to pursue the compact course, changes to the bigger Hudsons had to be limited—perhaps capping the ceiling on repeat sales to Hudson loyalists who wanted something new as well as limiting the line's appeal to new purchasers.

Of course, if the Jet *had* been a styling and a sales triumph, Hudson would have sold enough of them to finance a major restyling of its big cars. Frank Spring's brilliant Jet-based design for the Italia showed what was possible.

But Ed Barit had a different idea for the Jet—a tearful Frank Spring was later to disown all responsibility for the Jet once Hudson management had had its way. Barit, like his contemporary, K.T. Keller at Chrysler, believed people liked to sit straight up in their cars, with hats on, of course. He liked high fenders, thought the step-down was too low, admired the interior arrangement of the Fiat 1400, and was fascinated with the Oldsmobile 88's rocket taillights. And, Barit wasn't the only Jet influence to give Spring the fits.

Chicago Hudson dealer Jim Moran also got his two cents worth. Moran was the company's biggest dealer. He moved 3,000 cars a year, nearly 5 percent of the firm's volume. When this man spoke, apparently everybody at Hudson listened.

Moran thought the '52 Ford was a worldbeater—he later became a Ford dealer. *Special Interest Autos'* founder, Michael Lamm, detailed the Hudson Italia saga in *SIA* #8. Mike learned that Moran apparently convinced Hudson's Sales vice president, Norman K. VanDerZee, that the Jet would only succeed

Far left: Parking lights blend smoothly into Jet grille. **Left:** *Roof-mount radio antenna can be flipped down for tight spaces.* **Below:** *Jet also carried one of the great styling cliches of the fifties, a fake airscoop on the hood.*

if it looked like a scaled-down Ford.

Frank Spring did a last-minute redesign on the Jet's rear window to ape the new Ford after PPG told Hudson they could supply wraparound rear windows if they conformed to the '52 Ford's curvature. This and Spring's other body refinements on this theme created an erroneous legend that Murray Body Corp. had developed the Jet body dies from cut-down Ford dies.

It's a pity when you consider what Frank Spring originally had in mind. The first Jet renderings incorporated many of the Italia's delightful styling features—a dramatically sloped hood and deck, low fenders with airscoops over the lights, smoother, more rounded lines, and doors which cut into the roofline.

After the interruptions from Barit, Moran, and the influence of a certain "Fiat 1400" (actually a mockup with a Fiat nameplate as a "disguise") in the engineering department, the Jet emerged as we know it. Vestiges of Frank Spring's original concept remained in the hood and deck lid creases, but in precious little else. The car was three to four inches higher than Spring intended, too.

When you recall that the sleek Italias were built basically from Jet components, it's not hard to imagine the design that might have been a turnaround for Hudson—just as the earlier stepdowns had been one of the smartest things on the road in 1948. The Italia was built partially to pacify Frank Spring and keep his interest in the company. He was ready to quit when the Jet reached its final design stage.

The new Jet stood an inch higher than the contemporary Wasps and Hornets (nearly 7 inches taller than a dramatic

Loewy Studebaker) and, despite its unit construction, the Jet weighed a whopping 2,700 pounds—200-300 pounds more than the Willys, Rambler, and Henry J. The car's height provided a lot of interior space—vertically—but very little rear seat leg room.

Remember, Hudson engineering was famous for building its cars like tanks. Their cars' weight and relatively high cost to build stemmed from a rule that seemed to insist on a series of bolts when just a few clips might have been sufficient. Chief engineer Milton Tancray's Jet design boasted 5,000 welds in each Monobilt body. With all that weight, the Jet needed every bit of its powerful engine to guarantee, as the showroom literature cooed, "When you put your foot down, something happens!"

The Jet's little 202-cid six, often erroneously called a scaled-down Hudson H-145 engine, shared the same pistons as the discontinued Commodore straight 8. Prudently, Tancray's decision to use existing tooling, less two cylinders (see sidebar, page 75), created a long-stroke six. *Road & Track*'s June 1953 Super

Jet road test discussed the advantages of this unconventional step "backwards."

The engine's small bore contributed to light reciprocating weight, so rod bearing loads weren't much different from a big-bore, short-stroke engine. The design also provided higher thermal efficiency and permitted higher compression ratios. John Bond wrote that 7:1 was the limit for a square engine, but Hudson's small bore "...gives the L-head combustion chamber an extended lease on life because compression ratios of 8:1 or more can be used without sacrifice in volumetric efficiency." Finally, Bond reasoned that the piston speed of a long stroke engine was a "negligible" factor In conjunction with overdrive or dual range HydraMatic.

On the road, Bond was impressed. "During the tests," he wrote, "we found that valve bounce occurred at an indicated 70 mph in second gear or 62.5 actual mph. This is 5,500 rpm, equivalent to a piston speed of 4,350 ft/min. During the performance tests we approached these speeds at least 75

Hudson Production —The Jet Era

1953	**1-2C Jet**	**4-5 Wasp**	**7-C Hornet**	Total Year
	21,143	17,792	27,208	66,143
1954	**1-2-3D Jet**	**4-5D Wasp**	**6-7D Hornet**	
	14,224	11,603	24,883	50,660
'53-54 Total	35,367	29,395	52,091	

Source: Adapted from *Hudson The Postwar Years* by Richard M Langworth, page 28

HUDSON JET

times and the little stroker was still running as smoothly and as quietly at the end as at the beginning."

In recalling that road test, John Bond told *Special Interest Autos*, "Bill Corey wrote our "Tune-Up Clinic" and was a strong Hudson rooter—even stronger than me. It was Bill who conned 'Genial Johnny Lail,' the Glendale [California] Hudson dealer into loaning him and later letting *R&T* road test the Jet.

"Bill came roaring up to our office, all smiles, and said, 'let's go!' So off we went, me driving. It was about 5 o'clock in the evening and our test strip was at Newport Beach, about 60 miles from Glendale. We had a quarter-mile strip measured and used red reflectors on stakes for after-dark testing.

"The first step was always speedo-calibration. I did this with Bill on the watches and the error was considerable.

But Bill wanted to do the acceleration

tests, so I agreed and he did the driving. I have never seen such brutal driving, and very much to my surprise that little stroker really stood up. It was running like a quiet little watch when Bill returned it to the dealer."

If the standard 104-bhp engine weren't enough, an optional aluminum head added another two horsepower, and that jumped 8-bhp more if Twin H-Power was fitted. A few 110-bhp Jets were supplied with dual carbs, but sans the high-compression head. Whatever the combination, Jets could leave their competition, and the rest of the low-priced three, far behind. The 114-bhp Twin H version had 23.6 lbs/hp—compared with 30.6 for the Rambler and 34.0 for the Willys 6.

The Ford V-8 weighed in at 30.0 lbs/hp, and a comparison check of contemporary road test figures shows that a Jet jockey could out-accelerate any 1953 Ford and had a top speed of nearly 10 mph more.

Jet brochures encouraged buyers to

select from HydraMatic or standard with optional overdrive—and then choose from four different rear axle ratios "...for the one best suited for your driving needs." Probably dealers in mountainous areas specified the 4.10 ratio; on the other end of the scale, overdrive with the 4.27 ratio was the most economical.

Jet sales in 1953 did nothing to prevent Hudson's steady decline. Wasp and Hornet sales results, due In a large part to the car's relatively unchanged appearance, dropped 20 and 25 percent respectively. Hudson had canceled the Pacemaker and Commodore sixes—and the Commodore eights. Unfortunately, the Jet's first year volume of 21,143 units didn't even help the firm to meet its '52 totals. Overall units fell by nearly 4,000 (less profitable) cars.

Although the first half of the year had started with a rush, it was mainly because Hudson's production planners had optimistically built nearly two thirds of the year's production by June. Hudson had even announced a small first-quarter profit.

The euphoria was short-lived. Outside factors piled up to thwart the Jet's debut. Hudson, along with other manufacturers, was plagued by wildcat strikes, interrupted by parts and material shortages, left waiting in line for GM HydraMatics when the plant suffered a fire, and harassed by the infamous "Ford Blitz"—it was about as much as any company could stand.

Nineteen fifty-three was a growth year for the industry, because this was the year Henry Ford II chose to seriously challenge Chevrolet. His strategy was simple and diabolical. He loaded up Ford dealers with more cars than they had ordered. The dealer force responded to a full pipeline by drastically discounting inventories to clear their lots. As fast as they did it, the transporters arrived with more cars. GM responded, of course, meeting the price cuts with more price cuts. The independents, and Chrysler, could only watch helplessly.

When the price war ended, nearly all the industry rankings had changed. Ford had crept within 17,000 units of Chevrolet; both had spectacular sales years. Buick and Oldsmobile had

Hudson Jet Options

Hudson offered a wide range of options for its Model 1C (Jet) and Model 2C (Super Jet) including four different axle ratios, two wheel widths, and seven tire selections.

Lots of color choices made Jet paint and trim selection a real showroom challenge. There were four basic shades, then Super Jet buyers could choose from four additional "special gem-lustre colors." For an average of $30 extra, these could be parlayed into a choice of 19 two-tone varieties. Love those old shade names—how about a combination of Robin's-Egg and Blue-Grass greens?

A trip through the rest of the 1953 option list, with a blank check, could easily add up to big money. Performance buffs could specify the aluminum 8:1 compression cylinder head ($13.75), Twin H-Power ($85.60), and combination fuel and vacuum pump ($11.11)—backed by stick with overdrive ($102.46) or HydraMatic ($178.03).

Then, picking selectively, oil bath air cleaners, an oil filter, an electric clock, deluxe eight-tube radio, tinted glass, "Weather Control" heater, and custom wheel discs left shoppers very little change from $300—and if you specified hand-buffed, genuine leather upholstery at

$136.57, you practically had a miniature Buick!

In 1954, the Jet-Liner had even more options. To make your Jet a junior Hornet, you chose from a list even longer than the '53s—and now it included Hornet wheel covers, steering wheel, continental kit, and even a Hudson-ized set of Kelsey-Hayes wire wheels. The wires cost $270 and must have been a rare option, indeed.

Hudson called the Jet-Liner, "The most luxurious car in the lowest price field." Owners who specified Plasti-Hide upholstery and trim (a version of Naugahyde) sat on reinforced, foam-rubber seats surveying the road from behind Hudson Teleflash signals on an instrument panel color-keyed to their Jet's interior. As the showroom brochure said, "Behind the wheel of a Jet-Liner, you're in for luxurious driving!"

On the utilitarian side, Jets could be fitted for police and taxi work. A special price list offered a heavy duty clutch for $3.75, a beefed-up generator and battery ($45.48), and heavy-duty shocks ($5.35). Finally, for those long hours on stakeout, or sitting at the taxi stand, beefy operatives could specify stiffer front seat springs by paying only $2.14.

specifications

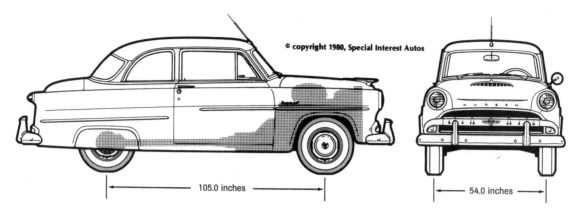

© copyright 1980, Special Interest Autos

← 105.0 inches →   ← 54.0 inches →

1954 Hudson 2C Super Jet

Price when new	$2,120 f.o.b. Detroit, Mich.
Optional equip.	Overdrive, special paint, high-compression head, Twin H-Power, HydraMatic transmission, fuel and vacuum pump, radio, tinted glass, heater, radio, leather upholstery, oil filter, Hornet appearance group, wire wheels, deluxe wheel covers.

ENGINE

Type	In-line L-head 6, chrome-alloy block, water-cooled, 4 main bearings.
Bore x stroke	3.0 inches x 4.75 inches
Displacement	202.0 cubic inches
Max. bhp @ rpm	104 @ 4,000 std (114 @ 4,000 optional)
Torque @ rpm	158 @ 1,600
Compression ratio	7.5:1 std (8.0:1, aluminum head).
Induction system	1-bbl downdraft (optional 2 1-bbl downdraft).
Exhaust system	Cast-iron manifold, single exhaust.
Electrical system	6-volt, battery/coil.

TRANSMISSION

Type	3-speed manual, column shift, overdrive optional (4-speed HydraMatic optional).
Ratios: 1st	2.605.
2nd	1.630.
3rd	1.000.

Reverse	3.536. (Automatic—GM 4-speed HydraMatic: 1st - 3.8195; 2nd - 2.6341; 3rd - 1.450; Rev - 4.3045).

CLUTCH

Type	Molded dry plate.
Disc diameter	9.125 inches.
Actuation	Mechanical, foot pedal.

DIFFERENTIAL

Type	Hypoid.
Ratio	4.10, 4.27 w/overdrive, also 3.31, 3.54 HydraMatic).
Drive axles	Semi-floating

STEERING

Type	Gemmer worm and roller
Ratio	20.2:1
Turns lock-to-lock	4.2
Turn circle	33.4 ft.

BRAKES

Type	Centrifuse iron drums.
Drum diameter	9.0 in.
Total swept area	132.14.

CHASSIS & BODY

Frame	Monobilt unit body and frame; all steel box section.
Body construction	All steel.
Body style	2-door, 6-passenger sedan.

SUSPENSION

Front	Unequal length A-arms, coil springs, tubular hydraulic shock absorbers, stabilizer bar.
Rear	Solid axle, semi-elliptic leaf springs, tubular hydraulic shock absorbers.
Tires	5.90 x 15 std (optional 6.40 x 15).
Wheels	4.00 x 15 std (optional 4.50 x 15).

WEIGHTS AND MEASURES

Wheelbase	105.0 inches.
Overall length	180.687 inches.
Overall height	62.75 inches.
Overall width	138.375 inches.
Front tread	54.0 inches.
Rear tread	52.5 inches.
Ground clearance	7.4 inches.
Curb weight	2,838 pounds.

CAPACITIES

Crankcase	5.0 quarts.
Cooling system	15.0 quarts.
Fuel tank	16.0 gallons.

FUEL CONSUMPTION

Best	22-24 mpg.
Average	18-20 mpg.

MARQUE CLUB	Hudson Essex Terraplane Club
Address	23104 Dolorosa St. Woodland Hills, CA 91364

---

shouldered past Plymouth, and the rest of the independents slipped behind Cadillac's tenth place finish. The "Blitz" pretty well finished the independents. The year 1955 would see all of them forced to merge to survive, if only for a short while. Chrysler licked its wounds, borrowed $100 million, revamped its styling, and showed it had a few surprises left. For the rest, it was the beginning of the end.

Hudson slipped to fifteenth place, and was even passed by Packard. That ven-erable establishment was making a last-ditch sales drive, spurred on by its new president, James Nance.

Colossal expenditures overwhelmed Hudson management. Besides the big Jet tooling bill, which was incorrectly amortized on a unit basis against Murray's production, unsold inventories of all models piled up, Korean War defense commitments (Hudson built B-57 airframe components and B-47 spares) required cash outlays, and the company was plagued with the usual types of

Below: Oldsmobile influence shows in steering wheel and dashboard design.
Right: Rugged flathead six pumps out 104 hp at 4,000 rpm. Hudson's unusual cable-operated windshield wipers were carried over to the Jet. *Below: Unit body is well engineered. There wasn't a squeak or rattle anywhere in the driveReport car.*

HUDSON JET

operating losses and inefficiencies that hover around a business when its back is to the wall.

At year's end, Hudson had incurred its greatest loss ever, $10,411,060 on sales of $193 million.

As 1954 rolled around Hudson appeared for the seventh consecutive year with minor changes on its basic 1948 step-downs. With almost no money left, they'd had little choice. Still, the cars looked a bit different, with one-piece front and rear windshields, raised, squared-off trunks and subdued trim. The big Instant Action sixes (particularly the legendary 7X option) were quicker than ever. Hudson finally had power brakes and power steering—although road testers commented the first-year designs were no improvement over the excellent manual systems of prior years. Even a continental kit was available, but buyers failed to materialize.

The "new" Jets were only slightly different from the 1953s—the grille had raised bumps, while the Super Jets featured twin side spears that helped break up the slab sides visually, while adding to an impression of greater length. A low-priced economy model two-door called the Jet Utility Sedan came equipped with a fold-down rear seat for cargo storage that extended into the trunk.

Other changes for 1954 included redesigned combustion chambers so Jet engines could be called "Instant Action" like their Wasp and Hornet cousins. The rear seats were moved backwards two inches in response to repeated pleas for more leg room.

On the other end of the scale, the new series 3D Jet-Liner was years ahead of its time. The Jet-Liner, a miniature luxury version of the big Hudsons, could be

ordered with a host of trim, upholstery and luxury options—even steering wheels and hubcaps from the Hornet series to complete the look-alike pose. Hudson advertising positioned the Jet-Liner as "a compact version of the fabulous Hudson Hornet, US Stock Car Champion."

There wasn't much impetus in 1954 for the idea of a luxury compact. In the first place, gasoline was still five gallons to the dollar, and in the second, as very few takers were lining up for big Hudsons, still fewer wanted a "loaded" little one.

Undaunted, Hudson management had one last straw—the final Hudson-built model ever was announced in April 1954. As buyers weren't forthcoming for the top-of-the-line Jets, Hudson sought desperately to revive interest by offering the Jet Family Club Sedan—a low-priced car designed to undercut the low-priced three. The rather stark Family Club initially was available for $1,465—though it shortly rose to $1,600.

Sales Manager VanDerZee's brief to his salesmen was classic—and, to my recollection, not too different from the Willys Americar launch 15 years earlier. Hudson hoped the rock-bottom Jet would appeal to "millions of American

families without an automobile, and many more in need of an economical and dependable second car."

It was a sad way to finish. The Hudson merger with Nash-Kelvinator Corp. had been common knowledge the previous fall, just after the introduction of the 1954 models. Rumors were rampant that Hudson would be "orphaned"—that Hudson car production would be switched to the more modern Nash and Rambler offerings. It's hard to gauge the effect this had on sales of the '54s, but it certainly couldn't have helped buyer confidence.

The last of the 14,244 '54 Jets rolled off the production line on August 23, 1954. There would no longer be a need for a model with the Jet's specification now that Ramblers were being built under the same banner. The Jet engine powered the '55 and '56 Nash-bodied Wasps but was dropped the following year.

Conceptually, the Jet was sound—a powerful but economical light car, with a host of options—but its timing, and styling, couldn't have been worse. Could an Italia-styled Jet have been successful, we'll never know. I suspect that the economics of independent carmaking, in the face of an onslaught like the "Ford Blitz," would have doomed any effort to oblivion. The Jet lived on in spirit in the Ramblers bedecked with Hudson badges, but the proud and rugged sense of independence that was Hudson was soon gone for all time.

Driving Impressions

Ed Brown's '54 Super Jet has been in his family since it was purchased new in that year as a Christmas gift for his mother. It's an all-original automobile, and when we drove it the Jet was about to turn 55,000 miles.

The doors on the Jet really open w-i-d-e to welcome you in—the swing is close to

HUDSON JET

90 degrees and entry into the front seat is as easy as you'll ever find in a Fifties car. With optional foam rubber, the seats are quite comfortable and give chair-like support to your shoulders and thighs. The Jet didn't skimp on glass, either. Visibility in all directions is outstanding.

A quick turn of the ignition key puts the flathead six into action, and a smooth, quiet unit it is, very much in the Hudson tradition. Drop it into first and off we go. Gearshift action is a bit notchy but quite positive. The tranny is a Borg-Warner unit, according to Ed Brown, and he feels it's not up to Hudson-built standards. There's plenty of torque on tap through the gears, and acceleration from 35 to 55 in high gear is especially impressive, coming on smoothly, steadily, and quickly without any fuss whatsoever from the engine.

Brakes, however, are a different matter. They're probably no worse than the Jet's contemporaries but they're no better, either, requiring a high degree of pressure for half-hearted results. Steering effort is moderate at low speeds and light and pleasant on the highway. There's good directional stability, and the turning circle, in keeping with its short wheelbase, is very tight.

The biggest surprise the Jet handed us was its riding qualities. If you were riding blindfolded you'd swear you were in a much larger, heavier car instead of a 2,700-pound compact. Even the choppiest surfaces don't upset the Jet's or the passengers' poise, and a long-distance jaunt in this car must be a pleasure. Some body roll manifests itself during

Too Late To Do Much Good

Looking back to *Road & Track*'s June 1953 road test of the Hudson Jet, it occurs to me that this remarkable engine came 23 years too late. It should and could have been introduced in 1930!

Here's my version of the story. In 1928 or 1929 Hudson-Essex management and/or engineers decided that the magnificent F-head Super Six engine would have to go. It was bulky, heavy and costly to build. And the straight eight was the newest rage and seemed the way to go.

So what was more logical then to add two more cylinders to the Essex Six? Chief engineer Stuart G. Baits, in a rare stroke of genius, made one very important change in the layout of the 1930 Hudson Great 8 engine. Instead of using the Essex scheme of three main bearings with three cylinders hanging between each pair, he put in five mains with the cylinders in pairs. Actually, there was no other choice, except to go with three mains like the single-overhead-cam Duesenberg engine—and that would have been a godawful choice.

At the same time Hudson-Essex engineers also put a bit more lengthwise space in the block. This allowed for a future bore increase to 3 inches from the original 2-3/4 inches and also provided room for larger intake valves: 1-1/2-inch instead of the 1-3/8-inch intakes and exhausts used in the Essex.

The eight cylinder crankshaft was a massive, magnificent forging and was the first eight cylinder ever with integral counterweights. Splash lubrication was retained, but a new dual-acting oil circulation pump fed oil to opposite ends of the engine instead of only to the front as on all previous Hudson and Essex sixes.

My point is this: if only at the same time Hudson would have used the paired cylinders of the eight on the six, then the six would have had four mains and there, ladies and gentlemen, we would have the 1953 Jet engine! Of course, the Jet engine had full pressure lubrication, but only because Baits himself was finally overruled on this point.

John R. Bond

cornering but, again, not much worse than the competition in '54.

After 26 years the Monobilt body is still as tight as the proverbial drum, and the fit of the doors and trim is first-cabin throughout. The Jet may have been designed as a low-priced car but it certainly wasn't a cheap one. And with its compact dimensions, 25 mpg economy, comfortable passenger capacity, and gobs of trunk space it seems there's only one thing really wrong with Hudson's Jet. It was brought to market about 27 years too soon. 🐾

Acknowledgments

Secondary sources: Hudson, The Postwar Years, *by Richard M. Langworth;* Hudson's Four Wheel Jet, *by Wayne R. Graefen;* Car Classics 1974 Yearbook; The Jet, Hudson's Last Take Off, *by Robert C. Ackerson; Cars & Parts; Road Tests and articles from Automotive Industries, Road & Track, The Autocar, Motor Trend, Automotive News, Speed Age, and Hudson sales literature.*

Our thanks to John R. Bond, Escondido, CA; James Bradley, National Automotive History Collection, Detroit Public Library, Detroit, MI; and members of the Hudson-Essex-Terraplane Club. Special thanks to Ed Brown, Norwich, CT.

Top left: Jet's appearance is uncontroversial but pleasant. Above: Can you spot the error in the bill of sale for driveReport car? Below left: Jet will lean a-plenty on corners, but the chassis sticks surprisingly well. Below right: That high bustle trunk gives plenty of carrying room.

1954 Hudson Hornet

The Hudson Hornet was the safest, best handling car of its time, but that didn't stop its sales decline.

By Tim Howley

Photography by David Gooley

Driving Impressions

Our driveReport car is a very rare 1954 Hudson Hornet Special club coupe. This was the body style that was grabbed for racing, and this is the only one in Southern California that is known to have been restored. In this very last year, Hudson did some strange things with both the Wasps and the Hornets because they knew they were coming to the end and they wanted to lower the prices and use up all the spare parts. Lifelong Hudson lover Terry McClanahan, San Diego, California, bought this car about five years ago in Chula Vista, California. It was still in the hands of the wife of the original owner, a minister who had driven the car until he died. A friend of Terry's saw the car in the driveway all covered up and told Terry about it. At the time that Terry purchased the car it had about 83,000 original miles; it now has 90,800 miles.

McClanahan restored this car to be a driver, not a showpiece. The car had a minimum of accessories, Hydro-vac power brakes, heater-defroster, and Hudson hydraulic jack. It does not have Twin H Power because that was an option on the Hornet, and in keeping this car original he has decided not to add this item. The car has the standard hubcaps with optional beauty rings. The shields behind the door handles and gas cap cover were options that were originally on this car. There are optional bumper bars in the rear but not the front. The wind-up clock is standard. There never was a radio in this car. The Borg-Warner automatic transmission was used only briefly in 1954, due to a fire at GM's HydraMatic plant. McClanahan was fortunate enough to find another Hudson Club member who had a bolt of the original seat upholstery in green, same color as was in this car. So all of the checkered material that you see is the correct original material. The original spare is still in the trunk, and all of the replacement tires are the same, B.F. Goodrich Silvertown tubeless 7.60:15 white sidewalls, which are again being made. Note that the whitewalls were

options on this car when new.

The restoration was done about as far as one could go without going all the way down to the frame. The car was repainted and rechromed, stainless straightened and polished, and new interior and heads were installed; transmission, rear end, and engine accessories were rebuilt, but not a complete engine overhaul. When Terry finished the car he gave it to his wife Lynn for her birthday. When restored, the other Hudson he has will be Terry's car.

McClanahan's parents always owned Hudsons; they bought a 1949 Hudson in 1949; Terry learned to drive on a Hudson; his first car was a Hudson Jet; and he still has his parents' 1953 Hudson Hornet four-door sedan which they bought new. This will be his next restoration project. McClanhan owns American Hummer Supply, a Hummer service and accessories shop in LaMesa.

By 1954 standards this is an excellent handling and riding automobile. Steering is by armstrong, but Terry says the car has a good ratio and such a big

wheel that it is easy to steer under all conditions, except parking. Aiding the car's remarkable cornering ability are its extra-wide body, a stabilizer bar in the front, and a sway bar in the rear. The braking is excellent. Even by today's standards there is power to spare. The car keeps right up with modern Interstate traffic, can pass anything at will, and roars right up the long inclines at 75 mph; and remember, this engine has never been rebuilt. Terry has driven the car as fast as 98 mph.

We did not find the Hornet with a Borg-Warner automatic to be very fast (taking about 15 seconds to go from zero to 60 mph), but its top speed of 97.51 and its ability to sustain close to that speed in the corners made it the fastest stock car in America from 1951 to 1954, as noted by *Motor Trend*. Bill France, NASCAR President, told the Society of Automotive Engineers in 1952, "There's not a safer or better handling American car on the road today than the Hornet."

In March 1999, Terry went on the Hudson Club's Laughlin, Nevada, econ-

omy run, where he got 18.4 mpg. And that was driving the car 70-75 mph. We found the car as comfortable as a fifties sofa and nearly as soft. We experienced considerably less lean than with most cars of the era before ball-joint front suspension, and with the windows closed the old Hudson is nearly as quiet inside as a modern car.

The instrument pod looks very similar to that of the Hudson Jet. The speedometer is easy to read with orange lettering on a black field and white gauges for fuel and temperature; there are lights for amps and oil, as was pretty much the norm for the industry beginning in 1954. This car has a standard windup clock mounted in the instrument pod. The cigarette lighter has never been used; the preacher never smoked. The Borg-Warner automatic transmission, even though rebuilt, is not nearly as smooth as HydraMatics of the era which we have tested. The Borg-Warner has just low and drive, no drive two, but there is a park position; Hydramatic used reverse as park. Despite the

squatty windows inspired by the 1942-48 Buick, visibility all around is excellent, infinitely better than the 1942-48 Buick. We really couldn't find many faults with this car as engineered, or as restored.

Tom McCahill, in testing a 1952 Hollywood Hornet for *Mechanix Illustrated* in their October 1952 issue, summed up the car's superior handling better than I ever could when he wrote, "The Hudsons are not the fastest cars on the track, they are not the lightest, and they are not the leaders in the acceleration department. So what cooks? Hudsons are ripping the feathers out of all other brands on one simple but oh so vital point. They are America's finest cars from the very important standpoint of roadability, cornering and steering.

"On a half-mile, or mile-and-a-quarter track, the ability to corner, plus top balance and steering control, plus excellent brakes, are all Hudson needs to smother the rest of the country's output. The Chryslers are faster, and several cars

The wide grille on the '54 Hornet was inspired by its smaller brother, the Hudson Jet.

Tastefully designed trim and trunk handle are very simply but elegantly shaped.

CLUBS

Hudson-Essex-Terraplane Club
Norm & Lou Lovell, Membership Co-Chairmen
P.O. Box 715
Milford, IN 46542
Bi-monthly magazine
Note: There are no other specialized Hudson clubs such as for Hornets only, Step Downs only, Essex Only, Terraplane Only. There are 44 chapters of HET in the United States, plus Australia, New Zealand and South Africa.

such as the 88 Olds and Cadillac can out-accelerate them. But to stay with the Hudsons on a race course, these other cars must literally pull themselves apart in the corners while the Hudsons sail around with effortless ease. This same factor that makes them tops in stock car racing is also the reason why I rate the Hudson America's safest big automobile.

"A standard Hudson Hornet, with nothing added, is quite a hot babe but nothing too unusual. Top speed is between 96 and 97, and zero to 60 goes just a hair under 15 seconds, actually 14.7 average. The Teaguemobile I tested had a top of approximately 107 and did zero to 60 in 12.1 seconds.

"Hudson is America's best road car by far, in spite of its Queen Mary width, which I for one could do without. As I reported several years ago, the windshield is so far forward from the driver's eyes that you get the feeling you are

always coming out of a tunnel. This and a few silly blotches of chrome are all the bad points I could dig up. Actually, the Hudson is one of the finest automobiles built in America, regardless of price. It will match any American car in comfort, roominess and general appointments. If you like 'em big and tough, here's your dish."

And this all comes from the guy who swore on a stack of bibles that the 1953-55 Mexican Road Race Lincolns were America's best all around cars of the time. And this test reporter, who eats and sleeps and drinks 1956 Lincolns, agrees with Uncle Tom 100 percent on his appraisal of Hudsons of this era.

Living with a 1954 Hudson

If you are going to buy a collector car to be a daily driver you couldn't come up with a better car than a Hudson of this era. They are just really strong, dependable, powerful, economical cars that

adapt extremely well to today's roads, fuels, and driving conditions. There is enough room in the trunk to sleep in it; and there is enormous room in the back seat of the two- and four-door sedans, but not in the back seat of the coupes, and even the front seats of the coupes are a little tighter than the sedans.

Hudsons' low center of gravity and outstanding suspension make them excellent road cars even today. A Hudson will hold the road at 100 mph, if you can find a place to go that fast without getting caught. Also, Hudson had a center-point steering setup which did away with the long crosslink and connected each wheel through tie rods to the steering arm which was mounted on the front cross member. The Hudson virtually did away with the high-speed wheel shimmy common to most cars of its day. The system also made steering easier and isolated road motion in a manner that one wheel's motion did not affect the other's so much. However, just because Hudson had superior suspension in 1954 does not mean that a 1954 Hudson will have great roadability today. As in any 45-year-old car, the suspension usually needs to be rebuilt.

Terry has accumulated hundreds of Hudson parts over the years, which makes maintenance easier. But even if you do not have a lot of parts, procuring the mechanical parts you require should not be too difficult. There are plenty of new, NOS, and rebuilt parts around; there are several people in the Hudson parts business, and other Hudson owners are generally extremely helpful. As with any make, it is the trim parts that are the hardest to find, although in the case of the 1954 Hudson, lots of trim parts are interchangeable between models and with earlier years. For example, during this period there are so many differences in trim pieces for Chrysler and GM products that it will drive the collector nuts. Meanwhile, Hudson had only slight trim changes from year to year and many trim pieces were carried over or interchanged with various models. This makes it relatively easy for the Hudson collector to find trim for his particular car. Because there are not thousands of

Bill France, NASCAR President, stated in '52, "There's not a safer or better handling American car on the road today than the Hornet."

Hudson collectors, like Ford and Chevrolet collectors, most trim parts are available and at prices that won't break your bank account.

The windshield is the hardest item to find. Up until 1954 Hudson had the split windshield, and beginning in 1955 it was a different car. So this is a one-year-only windshield, and it is one of the very few windshields from the fifties that is not now being made. This is the standard windshield; Hudson in 1954 also had a windshield that was tinted at the top. Skirts were standard on the Hornet Specials; while not hard to find, they now cost about $800 a set. They are really small skirts compared to some other makes.

When we asked Terry what peculiar problems Hudsons had, he thought a moment and said, "Well, they went out of business." Well, they did have a problem blowing head gaskets, both on the tracks and on the streets. This was solved by applying aluminum paint to the head gaskets, which later resulted in aluminized heads for all makes. Hudson engine blocks were made of chrome alloy which, while costly, promotes extremely long engine life. They also had chrome piston rings. Even today, many Hudson engines do not need reboring. Piston rings were pinned in place, and Hudson claimed that it shared this feature with Rolls-Royce. The brakes were fitted with a mechanical back-up system in the event of hydraulic failure.

Terry does not like the bias-ply tires at all and says that if he had to do it all over again, he would put radials on the car. Otherwise, he will not change it from stock. A lot of Hudson owners put alternators and Pinto fuel pumps on their cars, but Terry would not do this. He feels that the Hudson Hornet will keep up with the pack, even today without modifications.

Hudson did not have a fully automatic transmission until 1951. Their semi- automatic Drive-Master transmission, 1948-51, was a complex vacuum-operated unit which proved to be troublesome. Super-Matic came along in 1950. This was Drive-Master with a high cruising gear. GM HydraMatic, first offered in 1951 on the Hornet and Commodore only, was their most reliable transmission beyond a standard transmission. In 1952 HydraMatic became available on all models, and Drive-

Hydraulic jack a very rare Hudson accessory.

Chrome trim enhances rear window shape.

Small fender skirts in the rear were standard.

The functional cowl vent provides fresh air.

Hudson Hornet Special lettering on glovebox.

Gauge panel in '54 similar to the Hudson Jet.

Master and Super Master were dropped. A Borg-Warner automatic was offered on some cars in 1954, due to the fire at GM's HydraMatic plant. While it is a good unit, it does not measure up to Hydra-Matic, and in restoring a 1954 Hudson you may want to switch to Hydra-Matic.

Hudson History in the late forties and early fifties

Perhaps no American car of the early post-World War II period achieved the spirit of World War II futuristic design dreams better than the 1948 Step-Down Hudson, which was essentially a semi-unitized car. With a height of only 60 and a fraction inches, it had the lowest center of gravity of any American car. A 1948 Hudson is now remembered for its role in the motion picture *Driving Miss Daisy*, a movie about an eccentric little old lady and her black chauffeur. The producers chose the right car because the people who shaped Hudson in the late forties and early fifties were an eccentric group; diversified, creative, off-beat, and a strange mix of adventure-

some and conservative at the same time. The president was A.E. Barit, who came from the old school of craftsmanship and penny pinching; yet the '48 Hudson was anything but a cheap, penny-pinching car. Vice President was Stuart Baits, a solid engineer who liked the athletic life. The chief engineer was Millard Toncray, a man very much in the mold of Baits. Frank Spring, head of styling, was an aeronautical engineer, but his influence with management was not quite what it should have been. The 1948 Hudson, styled under Spring's direction, was done by Arthur H. Kibiger, Robert Andrews, Arnold Yonkers, Arthur Michel, and Bill Kirby. It was a small and highly capable staff that produced the most innovative car of the late forties short of the ill-fated Tucker.

Hudson's design was nothing like what we have now in fully unitized cars, or even perimeter frame cars. (See *SIA* #134) The frame was actually three units. The center section consisted of boxed girders with the floor pans dipping about halfway down into the frame. So you didn't step all the way down to

enter a 1948 Hudson. You stepped only halfway down. The other two frame sections, which carried the front and rear suspension, were fairly conventional. The body and frame were only unitized in the thirties' sense of the term like the 1934 Chrysler Airflow and 1936 Lincoln-Zephyr, which had truss-bridge arrangements. The passenger compartment framework is only welded to the chassis at a few key points. In the modern unitized car, which actually began doing this with the 1958 Thunderbird and Lincoln Continental, the body and chassis are fully integrated as one structural unit.

Further contributing to Hudson's low silhouette were two propeller shafts and three universal joints. The brakes got a boost from a mechanical backup system. If the hydraulic system went out, the mechanical emergency brake was engaged when the brake pedal hit the bottom of the stroke.

For its day, the Step-Down Hudson was a marvel of engineering and the integration of engineering and styling. But it was engineered without benefit of modern computer technology, which meant that both the body and frame were at least a thousand pounds heavier than they had to be. Another drawback with the Hudson was that the firm was locked into building the same car for years. Hudson's basic body shell did not change until 1955, after the merger with Nash to form American Motors. So a design that was very advanced in 1948 was quite out of date in 1954.

The 1948 Hudson had a tremendous public acceptance, with 117,200 units produced that year. The late Marshall Teague, who raced Hudsons so successfully, said that it was the safest and best handling car produced to date.

For 1948 Hudson introduced a new 262-c.i.d. six that had more displacement than the venerable 254-c.i.d. L-head eight, which had been around since the thirties. It was the first Hudson engine to feature full pressure lubrication. For 1948 there were two series: the Hudson Super Six and Super Eight, and Commodore Six and Eight, both on

1954 HUDSON MEMORIES

I had almost forgotten about Hudson Hornets until I saw our driveReport car.

Then suddenly I cried out to the photographer and owner, "This is Jinny McCoy's car!"

They both looked at me, dumbfounded. In 1957, while attending the University of Minnesota I briefly dated a campus queen named Jinny McCoy, or should I say she dated me. Jenny owned a two-tone blue Hudson Hornet club coupe, I believe it was a 1953 model. She considered this car far superior to any car owned by any guy she dated. Hence, you did not pick up Jenny in

your 1955 Chevrolet Bel Air or 1956 Ford Crown Victoria. She came to your place of residence in her hot Hornet. On about our third date I told her that I thought Hudson Hornets were kind of strange cars and this was a strange dating arrangement. I told her that on our next date I would pick her up in my coral and gray 1955 Chevrolet—and that was the last time I saw Jinny McCoy until several years later when I was married and she came to a party at our home with a new boyfriend. I asked her where her Hornet was and all I got was a cold stare.

Inline 262-cu.in. Six makes 160-hp at 3,800 rpm and 260-lb.ft. of torque at 1,800 rpm.

a 123.88-inch wheelbase. The Pacemaker was added November 18, 1949, nearly three months before standard Hudsons were introduced on February 10, 1950. Hudson added the Pacemaker in order to better compete with Pontiacs, Olds 88s, Buick Specials, Mercurys, and Dodges. The Pacemaker had a 4-inch-shorter wheelbase than the standard Hudsons, and the overall length was 6-1/2 inches less, all of it taken out of the nose. The engine was basically the Super Six destroked half an inch to go from 262 to 232 cubic inches. The carburetor was only one barrel. Rather than cutting into the competition's sales as was hoped for, the Pacemaker seemed to cut into Super Six sales as that series production declined from nearly 50,000 in 1948 to slightly over 17,000 in 1950.

The Hudson Hornet came in 1951. This was a Commodore with a special high-performance six-cylinder engine and Hornet badging. In the 1951 Hornet, the cubic-inch displacement of the six grew to 308 cubic inches, and the high-compression heads afforded a 7.2:1 compression ratio to make it by far the largest six in the industry. Horsepower was 145. (Hudson never had a V-8 until it became a part of American Motors in 1955, and by then it was too late.) Contrary to popular belief, Twin H-Power was never standard equipment on the Hornet. It came as an option on all six-cylinder models except the Pacemaker, beginning in 1952. Twin H-Power consisted of the earlier "Power Dome" cylinder head, plus a dual car-

1954 HUDSON HORNET SPECIAL CLUB COUPE MODEL 6D

PRICE	$2,619 f.o.b. factory, plus federal excise tax	**TRANSMISSION**		**SUSPENSION**	
Optional equipment	Power brakes, Borg-Warner 3-speed automatic transmission, heater, white sidewall tires, rear bumper bars and crossbar, wheel rings, exhaust pipe deflector, stainless steel decorations on back of door handles and surrounding gas tank filler door.	Type	Borg-Warner 3-speed automatic	Front	Independent unequal A-arms, coil springs
		The HydraMatic was 4-speed		Rear	Longitudinal leaf springs, sway bar
				Shock absorbers	Double-acting hydraulic tubular
		DIFFERENTIAL		Tires	7.60 x 15, 4-ply whitewalls
		Type	Hypoid, Hotchkiss drive	Wheels	Pressed steel, drop center safety rims
		Ratio	3.58:1		
		Drive axles	Semi-floating		

STEERING	
Type	Worm and roller
Ratio	Variable
Turns lock-to-lock	5.75
Ratio	20.4:1
Turn circle	42 feet

WEIGHTS AND MEASURES	
Wheelbase	123.88 inches
Overall length	208.1 inches
Overall width	77.1 inches
Overall height	60.38 inches
Front track	58.5 inches
Rear track	55.5 inches
Ground clearance	8 inches
Shipping weight	3,505 pounds

ENGINE	
Type	L-head, 6-cylinder, in-line, chrome alloy block
Bore x stroke	3-15/16 inches x 4-1/2 inches
Displacement	262 cubic inches
Max. bhp @ rpm	160 @ 3,800
Max. torque @ rpm	260 @ 1,800
Taxable horsepower	34.9
Compression ratio	7.5:1
Pistons	Aluminum alloy
Main bearings	4
Valves	L-head
Lifters	Solid
Induction system	Single downdraft carburetor, camshaft pump
Lubrication system	Pressure
Exhaust system	Single
Electrical system	6-volt

BRAKES	
Type	4-wheel hydraulic drums, internal expanding, with mechanical emergency reserve
Drum diameter	11 inches
Total swept area	158.7 square inches

CHASSIS & BODY	
Frame type	Boxed and channel-section steel integrated with body
Body construction	Semi-unitized, all steel members
Body style	Club coupe

CAPACITIES	
Crankcase	7-1/2 quarts
Cooling system	18.5 quarts
Fuel tank	20 gallons
Fluid drive	11 quarts
Differential	3.5 lb.

PERFORMANCE	
0-60	12.1 seconds
Top speed	107 mpg

Source: Tom McCahill, *Mechanix Illustrated*, October 1952.

Deep bench seat provides good thigh support.

Instruments easy to read through big wheel.

Deep trunk houses the original spare tire.

Nicely upholstered door panels.

HUDSON'S RACING GLORY DAYS

In 1951 Hudson introduced the Hornet with a 308-cid, 145-hp engine. While not the largest or most powerful engine in the industry, it was combined with the best roadability of any American car, plus it was the safest car on the tracks. This car was the package that could cream the crop, and the top NASCAR drivers soon found it out. Hudson, absent from the leading cars in 1950, suddenly emerged as the third place victor in '51, behind Olds and Plymouth.

Hudson's luck began at Daytona Beach in February. The winner and soon to be lead driver for Hudson was Marshall Teague, a burly, affable service station operator in Daytona Beach. A Jacksonville, Florida, Hudson dealer had offered Teague the car for the race. Teague, in turn, took the Hornet to his garage, tore down the engine, loosened all the clearances, and readjusted the valves and ignition timing. Shortly after blowing everything away at Daytona, Teague was invited up to Detroit where Hudson gave him two new Hornet coupes to race, one with standard transmission and one with Hydra-Matic, plus a third Hornet to use as a tow car, and $1,000 a month for as long as Teague competed with Hudsons. Hudson also assigned a young engineer, Vince Piggins, to oversee Hudson's racing activities. Any prize money was Teague's to keep, and a substantial advertising budget was allocated to promote Hudson victories. That first season Hornets won 13 major NASCAR races, and Hudson emerged in third place behind Olds and Plymouth. Teague won five of these races; Herb Thomas another five; Figaro, Rathman, and Flock one each. Thomas joined the Hudson team in August 1951, switching from Olds 88s and piloting the HydraMatic Hornet

while Teague drove the stick shift job. Those "Teaguemobiles" were worked over to the max, and Twin H-Power, which was not available from dealers until mid 1952, was employed by Teague for some of his later races with 1951 models but was eventually ruled out. Teague also entered a Hornet in the 1951 Mexican Road Race. It was definitely the fastest and possibly the nearest to stock car in the race, but Teague had a lot of bad luck and finished sixth.

In 1952 Teague left NASCAR and joined AAA which later became USAC. That year seven stock cars had the edge over Hudson in horsepower, but none could take the Hornet in the turns. That year saw the Hornet rack up 27 NASCAR victories, while its nearest challengers, Oldsmobile and Plymouth, could do no better than three wins each.

Adding AAA, the number of Hudson victories rose to 49.

In 1953 Hudson won NASCAR 22 times—two victories above the Oldsmobile record in 1951. Total number of victories were 46. In 1954 it stood third in the list of winning cars with 12 checkered flags to Herb Thomas. He was beaten by Lee Petty in a 1954 Chrysler who took seven first places but scored higher overall in point standings. Other Hudson drivers accounted for five more firsts that year.

In 1955 Hornet went from the unbeatable Step Down Design to a Nash body with a Packard 235 hp V-8. Above 60 the front wheel bounce was heavy and the steering lost its bite. Meanwhile, Hudson's competitors had tackled their own suspension problems with aplomb. That year 1953 and 1954 Hudsons still won some races, but it was nothing compared to earlier years.

buretor induction system with dual intake manifolds.

The Hudson Wasp came in 1952 on a Pacemaker platform, with the Pacemaker's 119-7/8-inch wheelbase, then added the 262-c.i.d. six-cylinder engine, developing 127 hp as compared to the Hornet's 145 hp. Soon after the Wasp's introduction, the Pacemaker virtually disappeared for lack of buyers. 1952 was also the last year of the Commodore six- and eight-cylinder models. In fact, after 1952 no eight was offered. In 1953 the Pacemaker was discontinued completely with the expansion of the Wasp into the Super Wasp Series and the introduction of the Hudson Jet. The Jet was a new mid-sized car on a 105-inch wheelbase. Late in 1953 a new Hornet option was added, a super-high-performance engine called the 7-X. It put out 200 hp or possibly even more. On May 1, 1954, when Hudson became a division of American Motors, the Hudson Metropolitan four was added. The Twin H 308-cubic-inch was offered through 1956, but was seldom opted for when Hudson now offered a 208 hp Packard V-8.

1954 Hudson Hornet Special History

The 1954 Hudsons were introduced October 2, 1953. These were the most extensively restyled Hudsons in the seven-year run of the Step-Down Design. Under Frank Spring's direction, the bodies were completely reskinned, giving them a more contemporary look and taking styling cues from the Hudson Jet. The 1954 Hudsons had what copywriters coined "Flite Line Styling." Higher rear fenders were now welded to the body. These new fenders gave the rear end a higher look, with taillights at the top of the fenders rather than at the bottom. The higher fenders were accented with more bustle to the trunk. The new grille took its cue from the Hudson Jet, the hood was flatter/bolder and had a wider and functional air scoop. While the look was contemporary, the design did not fool buyers who knew it was still the same old 1948 model underneath. A V-8 in 1954 might have given Hudson a second chance. But there was neither the money nor the interest in Hudson's entering the V-8 world.

On January 14, 1954, Hudson directors approved a merger with Nash-Kelvinator. Hudson stockholders approved the merger on March 24. On May 1, Hudson officially became a part of the newly formed American Motors. The last models introduced by the venerable and independent Hudson Motor Car Company of Detroit were the Hornet Specials, which appeared on May 19, 1954. They were an attempt to use up spare parts and lower the price because Hudson knew that its days as an independent with the Step-Down design were nearly over. The Hornet Specials did not sell well; many dealers still were overstocked with them when the 1955 Nash-Hudsons arrived in the fall.

The Hornet Specials were more Spartan than the full-on Hornets and carried price tags of $115 to $140 less. They had Hornet Special badging on the front fenders, Hornet exterior trim, and Wasp interior trim. The body styles were not quite the same as the Hornet. The club sedan was only available in the Hornet Special and the Hollywood hardtop, and the convertible came only in the Hornet, not the Special.

All Hornets and Hornet Specials had 160-horsepower engines in 1954. The added horsepower over 1951-53 came from larger valves, a hotter cam, and a compression ratio boost from 7.2:1 to 7.5:1. Optional Twin H-Power raised the horsepower to 170. There is an emblem on the cars which have Twin H-Power. Standard features on the Hornet Special were a windup clock, custom wheel discs and skirts. Sedans and the club coupe were upholstered in 15% nylon worsted Bedford cloth with broadcloth bolsters and vinyl trim on the door panels. The only interior colors were brown, blue, or green. The convertible was offered in blue, maroon, and green genuine leather seats with vinyl door panels. The Hollywood hardtop came with antique white vinyl accented with red, blue, or green bolsters. The Hornet Special had handles on the back of the front seats, lap robe ropes, map pockets, but no assist straps on the centerposts.

While the trim choices were minimal, there was a staggering array of powertrain and convenience options. You could have a Borg-Warner automatic transmission or Borg-Warner overdrive. (Since fire completely destroyed GM's HydraMatic plant a few days after the 1954 Hudson's introduction, very few were installed.) There were power brakes, power steering, heavy-duty shock absorbers, heavy-duty springs, sunshade windshield with Solex glass, outside visor with traffic light viewer, windshield washer, hydraulic windows, safety group with or without backup lights, chrome-plated wire wheels, six or eight-tube radio, special paints, and special upholstery, but no air-conditioning. Terry's car has the exhaust deflector with the Hudson emblem, a $2 item in 1954.

Whatever Happened to Hudson?

The last Step-Down Hudsons rolled off the Detroit line October 2, 1954. Eleven days later the first Nash Rambler-bodied Hudsons came down the line in Kenosha, Wisconsin. It was a sad but necessary end. The unitized Hudson introduced for 1948 was a mixed blessing. While more solid, safe, and comfortable than its competitors, it was heavier and inherently more expensive to build.

Unlike prior models, the '54 taillamps were set into the top of the expansive quarter panel.

Hence, Hudson could not compete, dollar for dollar, with the several makes it rivaled. Moreover, it was so expensive to retool that Hudson was forced to stay with this same body for seven model years. They couldn't even add a station wagon or air-conditioning. In addition, Hudson lacked the resources to develop an ohv V-8. Sales remained strong through 1951 (see accompanying chart), then nosedived in 1952 and never recovered. Unfortunately, racing victories do not necessarily translate into increased sales. In the case of Hudson, sales declined sharply after 1951 despite impressive track performance in 1952, '53, and '54. The Hornet, like all Hudsons, was an expensive car. You could buy an Olds 88 with a V-8 for something like $500 less. What's more, Olds changed its styling for 1953, and Hudson did not. From 1952 on, the Hudson became somewhat of a cult car, and the cult was getting smaller all the time. The compact Hudson Jet, introduced in 1953, was of less than no help because it could not compete pricewise with Ford and Chevrolet. For the money spent on the Jet, Hudson could have developed a V-8! Nash bought Hudson not for its cars or engines, but for what was perceived as its strong dealer organization. Actually, the dealers were defecting to the Big Three. The party was over. The 308 engine was continued through 1956, and the Hudson name through 1957.

However, you can't blame Hudson's demise entirely on management's stupid mistakes, the biggest of which was the Hudson Jet. The times may have had more to do with the end of Hudson than anything. Those independents who made it through the thirties had a tough time once the post World War II car buying frenzy was over. Hudson did benefit from Korean War defense contracts, but these were suddenly cancelled when the war ended. Another factor: it takes just as much money for a small company like Hudson to build and market a car as it does for a giant like GM. Also, the Big Three had plants all over the country, Hudson produced cars only in Detroit. Then, in 1953, Ford and GM got into a price war and a sales blitz. In their efforts to bury each other they only buried the independents. Furthermore, there was always government interference, which hurt the independents far more than it hurt the Big Three.

While Hudson at AMC just trickled away, loyalty to the car has never died. Terry McClanahan comes from one of thousands of loyal Hudson families who refuse to let the Hudson go the way of the manual typewriter and the wringer washing machine. The popularity of Hudsons as collector cars today is a fine testimony to the superiority of these cars many decades ago. Hudson never built a bad car; they just wound up with a lot of bad luck. ෨

1954 HUDSON HORNET SPECIAL MODEL 6D MODELS, PRICES, AND WEIGHTS

Body Style	Factory Price	Weight
Four-door sedan	$2619	3560
Two-door club sedan	$2571	3515
Two-door club coupe	$2619	3505

Note: The two-door club sedan was only available in the Hornet Special while the Hollywood hardtop and convertible were only available in the Hornet, not the Special. Total production of Hornet Specials and Hornets was 24,833. There were no body style breakouts.

ITALIA... Hudson's

Hudson's Italia came from (and in some ways came because of) the little 1953-54 Jet. The Italia, in fact, was the Jet with most of its sedan superstructure lopped off and a new aluminum sport coupe body added in Italy.

To create Italias, Hudson shipped complete Jets across the Atlantic to Carrozzeria Superleggera Touring in Milan. Touring torched off and discarded most of the Jet's unit body, leaving only the chassis platform, cowl, and a bit of rear bracing. Suspension, engine, and running gear remained pure Super Jet. Touring then built up the aluminum 2-seater coupe body. (They also built at least one Italia-like 4-door sedan on a Hornet base.)

The Italia started as a mere glimmer in Frank Spring's eye. Spring, Hudson's styling director from 1931 to 1955, liked sports cars and always wanted Hudson to bring one out. When Hudson decided to go ahead with the Jet, Spring's initial styling sketches for it had much more of the Italia's flavor than the pinched, boxy, Ford-like lines that finally became the Jet. If Spring had had his way, the Jet would have been a much lower, sleeker, quite different car.

The Italia's history is largely the Jet's, so to understand the Italia, here's the Jet's background.

A. E. Barit, Hudson's president since 1936 (and with the company since 1910), liked head room and chair-high seats. Barit and Spring had gone round and round about the lowness of the 1948-54 Step-Down Hudsons. Spring wanted them even lower than they were, although at their introduction the Step-Downs were the lowest production cars on the road. Barit thought they were too low.

During the Jet's planning stages in the early 1950s, the wife of one of Hudson's top executives happened to be driving one of the larger Fiats—a tall, squarish car. Word has it that she mentioned to her husband that the Jet should have those same tall seats and high doors. She got her wish. During early testing, too, Hudson disguised Jet prototypes as Fiats.

Spring's initial styling drawings for the Jet had many of the Italia's touches: fender-mounted airscoops, sloping hood and deck, more rounded lines, and doors cut into the roof. None of these features reached production in the Jet. Instead, here's what happened.

A large Hudson dealer in Chicago had seen pre-production renderings of the Jet and urged Norman K. VanDerzee, Hudson's sales v. p., to make the Jet more like the 1952 Ford. This dealer had also apparently seen pre-production drawings of the 1952 Ford. VanDerzee easily convinced Barit, Barit convinced other management people, and they called in Spring. They had Spring completely revise his Italia-like Jet to make it look like a dehydrated version of the '52 Ford.

If you look at a Jet today, you'll see a horizontal crease in the hood about 2/3 of the way down its nose. This crease was Frank Spring's original hood line. Likewise, around back there's another crease in the decklid. It demarks Spring's original decklid height.

Barit liked the shape of Olds 88 tail lights, so the Jet copied those. Management raised the roof of Spring's original concept by at least three inches (figures vary), and this gave the Jet its scrunched look and flat body sides. Spring would never claim any responsibility for the Jet, and Bernie Siegfried, who worked at Hudson, remembers that after the Jet's mongrelization, ". . . I went up into Styling and saw Mr. Spring standing there with tears in his eyes, and I found out that he was kind of heartbroken because he had to give up on a car that he had his heart set on."

The Italia was thus born from four interrelated reasons: 1) Other auto manufacturers were coming up with sport and show models to gain

PHOTOS BY ROSS MAC LEAN & MICHAEL LAMM

Hudson shipped complete Jets to Milan, Italy, where Carrozzeria Touring cut off Jet superstructure, added aluminum Italia coupe body.

Last Fling

Super Jet in-line 6 with Twin-H delivers 114 bhp. This block was cleverly engineered so it could use old Hudson 8's boring equipment.

driveReport

By Michael Lamm, Editor

publicity, so it made sense for Hudson to do the same. 2) Hudson was long overdue for a complete restyling of its full-sized line, and management wanted to test public reaction to the Italia's general design and ideas. 3) Carrozzeria Touring was actively wooing Hudson, asking them to let the Milan coacbbuilder construct some show/sport models on a one-off or short-run basis. And 4), Hudson management might reasonably have felt a twinge of guilt at the way they'd put down Frank Spring on the Jet. They were ready to hand him a victory after his defeat with the Jet.

Representatives from Touring had come to the U. S. in the early 1950s with sketches, photos, and prices in hand. Their prices looked particularly good—much lower than anyone could offer in this country. Touring was able to quote such low rates because Italian labor was cheap, and in Touring's case, overhead was, too. Carrozzeria Touring, defunct now since 1967, had been building custom bodies for Ferrari, Aston, Lagonda, etc., and enjoyed a fine reputation.

The decision to go ahead with the Italia was corporate, but this time the design was mostly Spring's. Spring worked directly with the Touring people. Between Spring's staff and Touring's, they ironed out production details, and Spring made several trips to the Milan plant between 1952 and 1954.

The first Italia coupe was ready in mid-1953, and Spring went over with his wife, Clara, to see it being finished. This coupe differed in several details from "production" Italias—it had overdrive, a die-cast grille, and an entirely different dashboard. This car is now owned by Victor Racz of Allen Park, Michigan, one of Spring's best friends and an old motorcycling buddy.

Spring's second trip to pick up a car was with A. E. Barit's son, Robert, who was Hudson's purchasing v. p. at the time. Spring was taking delivery of the Hornet-based X-161 4-door that he would own until his death in 1959. Robert Barit recalls the trip: "It was January 1954. I remember the Touring plant vaguely as a hole-in-the-wall operation, down a narrow side street with a sort of production line snaking through a series of old dilapidated buildings which perhaps had been built for the purpose. I remember they had high ceilings, and the plant wasn't far from the *autostrada*. I also remember being taken for very fast rides both in our prototype and in something else very sleek, low, and sporty—a Lancia, I believe."

This sedan, dubbed the X-161, is now owned by a Hudson collector

Hudson Italia

in New York. Whether Touring built more Italia-like sedans isn't documented—some say there were four in all, others say only this one.

There's some disagreement, too, over the exact number of Italia coupes built on the Jet chassis. Most sources, including American Motors, say there were 25 ordered and 25 built. A few Hudsonuts maintain there were 25 ordered but only 19 built. We frankly don't know.

After the first Italia coupe was finished and shown, Hudson sent a letter (dated Sept. 23, 1953) to all its dealers inviting them to place orders for Italias at $4,800 f. o. b. Detroit. Apparently it was this letter that netted only 19 returns. Some Italias were sold in Europe and were never sent to this country.

Compared to GM Motorama show cars and limited-production sportsters like the Nash-Healey, Kaiser-Darrin, and even some of the fiberglass jobs of the time, Italias received amazingly little publicity. They were shown at all the major European salons, plus the big U.S. auto shows. Public reaction was mixed. Most people liked the Italia's general lines, but at the same time they felt the rear-fender organ pipes were rather gorpy. Whether Hudson would have used the Italia's styling on its post-1955 lines remains unanswerable.

Clara Spring, now living in Los Angeles, reminisces: "As you know, the Italia was Frank Spring's swan song. I cannot help but smile as I remember Frank returning home one night saying, 'Well, today I showed Mr. Barit my new design for the Italia's instrument panel.' Mr. Barit's remark was, 'It needs more flash, more sex appeal!' Frank always wanted to make his designs clean and simple, without extraneous ornamentation, for practical visibility, etc. We both had the relief of a good, quiet laugh."

From a cost standpoint, Hudson seems to have broken even on the Italia. Research and development came to only $28,000, one factory source told us. Stuart Baits, Hudson's first vice president and assistant general manager, views the Italia's overall economics this way: "If you're going to make two, you might as well go ahead and make 25. If you tool up for it once, the first one will cost you maybe $150,000. The second might be $20,000,

Italia has lockable storage bins in rear side panels. Slits in rear fenders duct air to brakes, as do eyebrow scoops above front fenders.

ROAD & TRACK

Gorpy fake exhaust pipes house stop/turn/backup lamps.

Doors curve into roof, ease entry, but windshield dogleg likes to bark kneecaps.

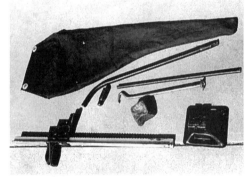

Carlo Borrani, also of Milan, supplied wires. Chromed fender indent plate gets nicked easily.

Italia's aluminum door handle fits flush, pops outward when you press thumb button behind it.

Tool kit includes lead cube to knock off wheel spinners; also plug wrench, U.S. bumper jack.

AMERICAN MOTORS CORP.

Jet instrument panel melts into special dash, with central glovebox, radio in front of rider.

Leather belts attach to seats. Firmness varies in bolsters. Seat can be moved 12 inches.

One original tire here. Trunk plus cargo deck inside gives Italia fantastic luggage capacity.

It looks good, performs beautifully, corners well. Jet suspension gives pleasant over-the-highway ride for comfortable high-speed touring.

THE MAN BEHIND THE ITALIA

When the woman fell asleep at the wheel, her foot pushed down the gas pedal and her Ford Station wagon lurched across the highway median and crashed head-on into Frank and Clara Spring's little Metropolitan

The Springs had been driving to Detroit, called by Roy Chapin, who wanted to talk to Frank about bringing out a hopped-up, sporty version of the Met. The accident ended Frank Spring's long and varied automotive career. He died on August 8, 1959, in a Claremore, Okla., hospital. Clara Spring miraculously survived.

Frank Spring had been what some people might call a health nut, a food faddist, a man who slept on the floor, a student of yoga and oriental philosophies. Incongruously, he also loved machines. Among his favorites were motorcycles—he owned a succession of Ariel Square 4s, big Vincents, and Triumphs. More often than not, he'd ride to work on a bike, even in the dead of winter.

He was also a great sports car enthusiast and aviation buff. At his death, he was restoring a 1936 BMW roadster, driving a gullwing Mercedes, and he owned the Hornet-based Italia X-161 sedan prototype. Clara Spring drove this car through 1980. Frank owned and flew a Beechcraft Bonanza.

Spring was a small, slight man with a European education and highly cultivated social manner. He generally got on well at Hudson and enjoyed his work. Whenever visiting dignitaries arrived from Europe or the Far East, Spring was called upon to entertain them.

Frank Spring was born in 1893, the only son (with four sisters) of a French mother and an extremely wealthy father. The Springs were an original California land-grant family, and it's said that at one time they owned most of the acreage between San Francisco and San Jose. The old Spring mansion and gardens still stand in San Francisco.

Frank's mother tended to spoil him, and he had trouble staying in American schools, so at age 12 he was sent to Paris. Here he had a private tutor, the young son of a Scottish laird, who took Frank on bicycling trips throughout Europe. When Frank became old enough, both he and his tutor bought motorcycles and toured the British Isles on them. Frank graduated from the Paris Polytechnic just before World War I, studying mechanical engineering and design.

During that war, he became an aeronautical engineer in the U.S. Signal Corps, assigned to aircraft production in Detroit. It was here that he learned to fly. After the war, he took a job with Paige-Detroit, designing and building engines. Then, after a short stint as chief engineer of the Courier Motor Car Co., Sandusky, Ohio (1922-23), Spring became general manager of Walter M. Murphy, Coachbuilder, in Pasadena, a post he held until 1931.

At Murphy, he supervised the design and construction of some of America's finest classics—Duesenbergs, the one-off Peerless V-16, Lincolns, Packards, Pierces, Minervas, Rollses, etc. He was also in on the ill-fated Douglas Dolphin, a competition-built airplane that eventually bankrupted Murphy.

In 1931, Spring moved to Hudson as director of styling. Here he had charge of all Hudson exteriors and interiors from 1933 until the company merged with Nash in 1954. During and after WW-II, Spring's department developed several radical idea cars, most of which came to nothing.

Steamer trunks fit here with ease. Stainless rub strips protect carpeting. Leather straps keep luggage from lurching forward in stops.

4-door Italia X-161 sedan was considered for future Hudson styling. Frank Spring's widow owned it until 1961. Car is now in New York.

TERRY BOYCE

Frank Spring hoped Hudson Jet would look more like this than the boxy thing it became. Drawing was made up from verbal descriptions.

Hudson Jet's unitized body/chassis included front subframe and steel perimeter, with recessed floor. Carrozzeria Touring left cowl but torched off roof and door pillars.

Excellent roadholding comes via Jet suspension and low cg. Race-winning Hornets had basically same springing.

Hudson Italia

second might be $20,000, and the third $5,000 and so on. As I remember, we about broke even on them—I think it about paid for itself on the whole deal."

The Italia project ended abruptly when Hudson and Nash merged in 1954 to form American Motors Corp. In the shuffle, Hudsons became Nashes, and it was Nash management who now called the shots.

We've managed to trace 15 Italias to their present owners in this country. Several more are reported to be in Europe, and at least one is in Africa.

Our driveReport car belongs to John J. Contus, an Inglewood, California, senior electronics consultant. He bought his Italia new in 1955 from a Santa Monica Hudson dealer. Mr. Contus had visited the Touring plant in Milan earlier that year, had seen Italias being built, and decided to buy one when he got back home. His car now has 36,000 miles on it, is original in every respect, and is No. 25 in the series—the last one built.

We slipped behind the Jet steering wheel and leaned back in the odd-shaped seats. They're made up in three sections—a bolster for the shoulders, another for the lower back, and a bottom cushion. Each section uses a different-density foam rubber (Frank Spring did some human factors studies and tested numerous seating ideas). We found the seats extremely comfortable—surprisingly so.

Another surprise: seatbelts. They're thick leather straps bolted to the seat itself, which means that in an accident about all they're good for is to hold up your pants. They're also slow to get out of, so we didn't use them.

The interior, as in all Italias, is done in red and white leather, with the dash crinkle-finished in red. It uses Jet instruments, but otherwise the panel is unique. Everything's in easy sight and reach, our only complaints being

that a car like the Italia should have full gauges, not warning lights, and that the radio should be nearer the driver rather than in front of the passenger.

Behind the seats, there's a huge open platform for luggage, with leather hold-down straps to keep cargo from shifting. Most likely, the Italia was originally planned for a small rear seat, judging by the decklid and the tremendous rear floor expanse, and the seat might have been scratched in a last-minute production compromise.

All Italias came with manual 3-speed transmissions, with column shift but without overdrive (except for No. 1). Mr. Contus's car ran and handled flawlessly, and while we'd expected some creaks and road rumble from the handcrafted aluminum body, we heard absolutely none. Precisely how the Italians grafted the aluminum onto the Jet's steel platform remains a mystery. There's a boxed member behind the trunk, and the recessed license plate rides inside this transverse box.

The Super Jet was a quick little car in its day, easily outrunning everything in its class plus quite a few bigger models. The Italia, being lighter and more slippery, is faster still. The twin-carbed flathead 6 revs willingly and strongly, and gears are well spaced for good acceleration in traffic. We'd estimate the Italia's top speed at 90-95 mph, because the Jet's was 88 despite its square body.

The Italia corners well, shows moderate lean, and the rear wheels will break loose predictably when shoved hard through corners. Ride is soft but not overly so—comfortable and stable at all speeds. The Jet's non-power steering feels a bit heavy and, like most, it's too slow for this type of car. Brakes are good, and at speed all drums have forced-air cooling.

Excellent visibility—all fender crowns are visible from the driver's seat. The windshield dogleg gets to be a knee buster at times, but not after you get used to the roof-cut doors and thus don't feel you have to stoop so much. We asked Mr. Contus whether rain drips down off the roof when he opens the doors, but he said no—that gutters catch it.

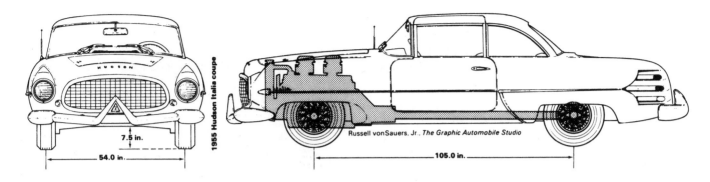

Russell vonSauers, Jr., The Graphic Automobile Studio

7.5 in.

54.0 in.

1955 Hudson Italia coupe

105.0 in.

SPECIFICATIONS
1955 Hudson Italia coupe

Price when new....... $4,800 f.o.b. Detroit (1955).

Current valuation*..... Xlnt. $9,500: good $,2000.

Options...........................Std. eqpt. includes flow-through ventilation, Borrani wire wheels, Twin-H-Power, aluminum head, anatomical bucket seats, leather upholstery, backup lights, seatbelts, day/night mirror.

ENGINE
Type .... L-head. in-line 6, water-cooled. cast chrome-
.... iron block. 4 mains. full pressure lubrication.
Bore &stroke .... 3.00 x 4.75 in.
Displacement............. 202 cu. in.
Max. bhp @ rpm ...... 114 @ 4,000.
Max. torque @ rpm .. 166 @ 2,000.
Compression ratio .... 8.0:1.
Induction system ...... Two 1 -bbl. carbs. mechanical fuel pump.
Exhaust system........ Cast-iron manifold. single muffler.
Electrical system ...... 6-volt battery/coil.

CLUTCH
Type...................... Single dry plate, woven asbestos lining.
Diameter.................. 9.0 in.
Actuation .... Mechanical. foot pedal.

TRANSMISSION
Type........................3 -speed manual. column lever, synchromesh.
Ratios 1st .... 2.60:1.
        2nd .... 1.63:1.
        3rd .... 1.00:1.
        Reverse............... 3.53:1.

DIFFERENTIAL
Type......................... Hypoid, open propeller shaft.
Ratio .... 4.10:1.
Drive axles............... Semi-floating.

STEERING
Type......................... Worm & roller.
Turns lock to lock ..... 4.0.
Ratio .... 18.2:1.
Turn circle.................38.5 ft.

BRAKES
Type......................... Drums, hydraulic, internal expanding.
Drum diameter.......... 9.0 in.
Total lining area........ 132.14 sq. in.

CHASSIS & BODY
Frame ....Unit chassis platform, hand-formed aluminum body.
Body construction..... Reinforced aluminum on unitized steel chassis platform.
Body style .... 2-dr., 2-pass., grand touring coupe.

SUSPENSION
Front ....Independent A-arms. coil springs, tubular hydraulic shock absorbers, torsional stabilizer bar.
Rear......................... Semi-elliptic leaf springs. tubular hydraulic shock absorbers.
Tires......................... 4-ply tube type. 6.40 x 15.
Wheels .... Borrani chromed wire wheels, knock-off hubs.

WEIGHTS & MEASURES
Wheelbase .... 105.0 in.
Overall length .... 183.0 in.
Overall height .... 54.0 in.
Overall width............ 70.0 in.
Front tread............... 54.0 in.
Rear tread .... 52.0 in.
Ground clearance..... 7.5 in.
Curb weight .... 1900 lb. approx.

CAPACITIES
Crankcase .... 5 qt.
Cooling system........ 16 qt.
Fuel tank .... 15 gal.

FUEL CONSUMPTION
Best .... 27.0 mpg.
Average .... 18.0 mpg.

PERFORMANCE (averages from **R&T, MT, Speed Age,** and **Auto Age** tests of Hudson Super Jet with Twin-H):
0-30 mph .... 3.97 sec.
0-40 mph .... 6.29 sec.
0-60 mph .... 13.66 sec.
0-70 mph .... 19.98 sec.
Standing 1/4 mile ..... 20.35 sec. & 68.6 mph.
Top speed................ 92.59 mph.

*Courtesy **Antique Automobile Appraisal**.

We were amazed at how well this Italia is finished—the obvious attention Carrozzeria Touring paid to small details. Other hand-built Italian customs we've driven, even the most expensive, showed generally poor planning and careless workmanship. Not this Italia. It's tight, with no major flaws and no bad habits. Good performance, admirable fuel economy, fine handling, great seating comfort for two, and a fantastic amount of luggage space make this a true Grand Touring car in the best international tradition. ဓဘ

Our thanks to J.J. Contus, Inglewood, California; Pete Booz, Victor Racz, Bernie Siegfried, Eddie Pock, Herb Malone, and Jack Miller of the Hudson-Essex-Terraplane Club, 23104 Dolorosa, Woodland Hills, California 91364; Clara Spring, Los Angeles; John Conde and J.J. Hartmeyer of American Motors Corp.; Robert Barit, Warwick, Bermuda; Stuart G. Baits, Grosse Pointe Farms, Michigan; H.M. Northrup, Grosse Pointe Park, Michigan; Carl Cenzer, Dearborn. Michigan; Millard Toncray, Onoway, Michigan; and Strother MacMinn, Los Angeles.

by Arch Brown
photos by Jim Tanji

1956 HUDSON

HORNET SPECIAL

IF 1956 was a memorable year in terms of automotive design, it was generally for the wrong reasons. Take the medium-priced field: The Buick, at least in its larger series, was bulbous. The Mercury had evidently been conceived by someone who had been struck by a chrome-plated lightning bolt. The Chrysler wore a conspicuously ill-fitting pair of fins atop its rear fenders.

And then there was the Hudson.

Or was there?

Hudson had merged with Nash in 1954 to form American Motors. Nash, which had most of the money and by far the best manufacturing facilities, became the dominant partner, and with the advent of the 1955 model year, Hudsons were manufactured in the Nash plant at Kenosha, Wisconsin.

They didn't look much like Hudsons, nor perform like Hudsons either, for that matter. The 308-cubic-inch flathead that had helped make Hudson a fearsome contender on the stock car circuit was still the base engine for the 1955 Hornet, and Hudson's famed "triple-safe" braking system was retained, but the chassis and body were pure Nash Ambassador—big and roomy, softly sprung, and very comfortable, but far too mushy for the racetrack.

Similarly, while the Wasp used the L-head engine of the late and largely unlamented Hudson Jet (see *SIA* #60), its body and chassis were those of the Nash Statesman. Nash aficionados refer to the hybrid Hudson as the "Hash." Some of the Hudson folks are gentler. They call it the "Hush."

Not that the situation was necessarily all bad, as we were to learn when we set about to prepare this driveReport.

Hudson had been very nearly on the ropes at the time of the merger. Sales had plummeted 75 percent in five years, and the development of the compact Hudson Jet had only served to further deplete the corporate coffers.

Nash, or more properly, Nash-Kelvinator, was somewhat better off. Thanks to Charlie Nash's frugal policies, which had been ably continued by his hand-picked successor, George Mason, the company was in reasonably sound financial condition. Sales were off, but not as drastically as Hudson's, and the Kelvinator division was a veritable gold mine.

Still, something had to be done, and quickly. The three-year-old Nash body shell would have to be updated with a wraparound windshield—*de rigueur* in those days—and some judicious (or possibly injudicious) rearrangement of the chrome trim.

A V-8 engine would have to be found, for the American motorist had had enough of medium-priced sixes. And a low-priced car would have to be provided for the Hudson dealers if they were to stay alive in a fiendishly competitive market.

The job was accomplished with remarkable dispatch. A deal was struck whereby American Motors would purchase V-8 engines from Packard, to be offered as optional powerplants in the Nash Ambassadors and Hudson Hornets. In return, Packard agreed to patronize American Motors' new stamping plant. Or at least that was how the AMC people saw it. Over at Packard the supplying of those engines was viewed—publicly, at any rate—as a favor magnanimously bestowed upon the struggling new American Motors. Within weeks, Packard purchased a stamping plant of its own, from Briggs. So much for reciprocity! (See sidebar, page 96.)

The principal advantage in the Hudson merger, from Nash's perspective, had been the acquisition of Hudson's dealer network. It was obvious that without a replacement for the moderately priced Jet, most of those dealers would go under, and it was equally apparent that the company had neither the time nor the money to develop a brand new car. The solution was as simple as it was—at least in retrospect—

obvious: Hudson nameplates were affixed to Nash's Rambler. It's a common practice now—witness the Aries/Reliant, Escort/Lynx, and Skylark/Omega twins, for instance—but the scheme was considered radical in the mid-fifties.

Meanwhile, a new V-8 was under development at AMC, a sturdy, overhead-valve job, capable of extracting more power per cubic inch than almost any stock engine then on the market. Measuring 3.5 by 3.25 inches initially, for a displacement of 250 cubic inches, the block was designed to handle a much larger bore, allowing for later increases in displacement without sacrificing coolant flow around the cylinder walls. Intake and exhaust port systems were also designed with an eye to future breathing requirements, and the crank-shaft, water, and oil pumps, main bearing caps and bolts, and connecting rods were all engineered for greater load-carrying capacity. Five main bearings and six counterweights were used.

All of which, of course, made the little 250-inch V-8 a highly efficient and nearly indestructible piece of machinery.

The purpose of the new engine was twofold: To eliminate AMC's dependence upon Packard as an engine source (and a good thing, too, given the subsequent

HUDSON, NASH OR HASH?

course of events at Packard!) and to provide the company with eight-cylinder cars to sell at a price well below that commanded by the Packard-powered jobs.

The preliminary announcement came in January 1956. *Automotive Industries* noted that American Motors was planning to market V-8 versions of the Nash Statesman and the Hudson Wasp. But when the cars appeared, three months later, the nomenclature had been changed. While the two newcomers did indeed use the 114.25-inch wheelbase of the Statesman and the Wasp, the more prestigious Nash Ambassador and Hudson Hornet titles were used, with the qualifier "Special" added.

The public's reaction must have been a severe disappointment to American Motors, for the new cars simply didn't fly in the marketplace. In their six-month selling season, only 1,757 Hudson Hornet Specials and 4,055 Nash Ambassador Specials were manufactured, and when the 1957 cars were introduced, both were conspicuous by their absence.

There were several reasons for the failure of the Specials, none of which had anything to do with their competence. First, by 1956 the body shell was in its fifth year, and this at a time when two- and three-year cycles were the norm for the larger producers.

Second, so far as traditional Hudson buyers were concerned, the Hornet Special wasn't really a Hudson at all; it was a Nash in drag! (They were quite right, of course. Apart from some of the trim, there isn't a single part or feature to be found on the car that is traceable to the Hudson Motor Car Company.)

Third, the Specials were over-priced

in relation to the competition. While their wheelbase and engine displacement were comparable to (and in fact slightly smaller than) the low-priced three, the Specials fetched a higher price than an Olds 88. AMC had a "Catch-22" situation here: In order to get the price down, volume would have to be increased, but in order to increase the volume substantially, a sharp price-cut would be required—something American Motors could ill-afford at that critical time.

But we were talking about styling. The 1956 Hudson may not have been the handsomest car on the road, but compared to most of its contemporaries it didn't come off too badly. The chrome-plated bib that served it for a grille was perhaps a little much, but

otherwise the brightwork was rather tastefully done—much more so, certainly, than that of the Nash. The full wheel cutouts looked better than the Nash's traditional skirted fenders, too, and they chopped three-and-a-half feet off the Hudson's turning circle while still allowing for a wider front track. But still, that warmed-over 1952 Nash body made the Hudson look dated.

Actually, to the motorist who wanted a big, roomy car that combined reasonably brisk performance with outstanding fuel economy, the Hudson and Nash Specials may well have been the cars of choice. In the 1956 Mobilgas Economy Run they delivered the most miles-per-gallon of any cars in their class, though the Olds 88 beat them out in ton-miles, the basis on which the event was scored.

Right: *If chrome was gold, the '56 Hudson would be a million dollar car.* **Below:** *"V" in rear door trim showcases Hornet name and V-8 emblem.*

New Passenger Car Registrations 1946-1957

Year	Industry total	Four	Hudson only**	% Independents	% Hudson**
1946	1,814,549	252,139	72,474	13.9	4.0
1947	3,166,337	336,150	83,344	10.6	2.6
1948	4,824,552	570,466	137,907	11.8	2.9
1950	6,308,157	651,325	134,219	10.3	2.1
1951	5,149,556	509,395	96,847	9.9	1.9
1952	4,128,035	445,199	78,509	10.8	1.9
1953	5,708,333	436,483	66,797	7.6	1.2
1954	5,499,295	245,845	34,806	4.5	0.6
1955	7,111,087	277,810	20,522	3.9	0.3
1956	5,853,195	212,758	11,822	3.6	0.2
1957	5,771,186	173,293	4,596	3.0	0.1

*Nash, Hudson, Packard and Studebaker
**Excluding Rambler

1956 HUDSON

(The Ambassador Special, at 20.71 mpg, was just a shade ahead of the Hornet Special's 20.49; while the Olds came in with 19.70.)

There was, by the way, one mechanical difference—in addition to the wider stance—between the Hornet version and its near-twin from Nash: The latter, which was priced a little lower than the Hudson, had solid valve lifters, while the Hornet variant came with the hydraulic variety.

Driving Impressions

Melvin "Red" Burke is unabashedly a Hudson man. "I've got seven of them," he notes. "It's kind of a disease, you know." In Red's collection, in addition to our driveReport car, are a '40 Traveler coupe, a pair of '47s (pickup and sedan), a '50 brougham, a '54 Wasp sedan, and a '52 Hornet that is presently undergoing restoration. The "disease" runs in the family. Red's son, Tom Burke, owns the '46 Hudson convertible that was a recent driveReport subject (see *SIA #72*).

The Hornet Special Versus the Competition

	Hudson Hornet Special	DeSoto Firedome	Mercury Monterey	Oldsmobile Super 88
Price*	$2,390	$2,393	$2,292	$2,363
Weights and measures				
Shipping weight	3,467 pounds	3,855 pounds	3,570 pounds	3,768 pounds
Wheelbase	114.25 inches	126.0 inches	119.0 inches	122.0 inches
Overall length	202.25 inches	217.9 inches	206.4 inches	203.3 inches
Overall width	78.0 inches	78.3 inches	76.4 inches	78.6 inches
Overall height	63.3 inches	62.7 inches	62.4 inches	62.3 inches
Engine				
Displacement	250.0 cubic inches	330.0 inches	312.0 inches	324.3 inches
Horsepower @ rpm	190 @ 4900	230 @ 4,400	210 @ 4,600	240 @ 4,400
Torque @ rpm	240 @ 2,000-3,000	305 @ 2,800	312 @ 2,600	350 @ 2,800
Compression ratio	8.0:1	8.5:1	8.0:1	9.25:1
Performance Factors				
Hp/c.i.d.	.760	.696	.673	.740
Pounds/c.i.d.	13.9	11.7	11.4	11.6
Pounds/hp	18.2	16.8	17.0115.7	

*Exclusive of federal excise tax and handling charges

Post-War Styling Cycles: The Independents vs. The Majors

Make	1947	1948	1949	1950	1951	1952	1953	1954	1955	1956	1957	1958
Hudson		7 Years							(See Nash)			
Nash			3 Years			6 Years						
Studebaker	6 Years						6 Years					
Packard		3 Years			6 Years				(See Studebaker)			
Chev/Pontiac			4 Years				2 Years		3 Years			1 Year
Buick		1 Year	4 Years				3 Years			2 Years		
Plymouth/Dodge			4 Years				2 Years		2 Years		3 Years	
Ford/Mercury			3 Years			3 Years			2 Years		2 Years	

As the above graph shows, during the Post-World War II period cars from the "big three" manufacturers received a major restyling more than twice as frequently as the "independent" makes. (Average intervals: 2.56 years for the "big three," 5.29 years for the "independents.")

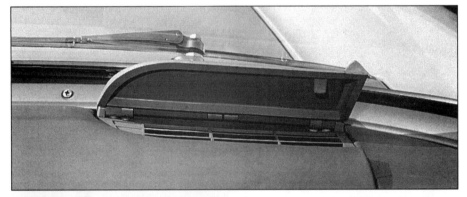

This one, the newest car in Burke's collection, is in remarkably fine, original condition. Red bought it in 1975 from its first owner, at a price so low that he prefers not to talk about it. The car's odometer registered 78,000 miles then, to which the Burkes—who are not inclined to treat their cars as museum pieces—have added another 10,000. Red replaced the valve lifters, but apart from that the engine has never been touched. The upholstery is original, as are the rubber floor mats—all in like-new condition. The chrome is all original too, and in beautiful shape, though the gold anodized radiator badge has been re-done, courtesy of a friend in the business, in 24-karat gold plate! Burke's only major expenditure on the Hudson was a fine new paint job, done in 1978 using the original (and very attractive) Crocus Yellow and Willow Green color scheme.

Red and his wife Edna have made two journeys to Los Angeles in their Hornet Special ("22 miles to the gallon, with the air-conditioner going most of the time," Burke recalls of their last trip). And they've taken it to club meets as far away as Reno, Nevada, and Vancouver, Washington. "It's a great road car," Red reports. "Very quiet and comfortable."

And indeed it is! We whisked the Hudson down a stretch of freeway, and at 65, in overdrive, the car seems to be loafing. Engine sounds are almost imperceptible, and even road noises are effectively muffled. We find it easy to believe Tom Burke's claim that the car

Above: Flip-up door hides A/C vent on dash. *Left:* Air conditioning also enters through low, wide cowl vent. ***Below left:*** Hudson's contribution to the parade of '56 fins. ***Below:*** Saber-style wheel covers are quite good looking.

1956 HUDSON

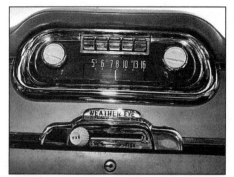

Right: Radio perches in center of dash along with Weather-Eye control panel.
Below: Speedo and gauges follow oval theme of radio.
Facing page, bottom: Taut handling of pre-AMC Hudsons was lost when Nash's cushy all-coil suspension was used on '55-'57 cars.

without strain at speeds in the low eighties.

Our personal transport, as it happens, is a European sedan with firm seats and taut suspension, so the "Hush" took a bit of getting used to. A good set of heavy-duty shock absorbers would go a long way toward eliminating some of the mushiness of this car's suspension, we're convinced. But having said that, we hasten to add that the solidly built Hornet Special glides along smoothly and softly, surrounding its passengers with an atmosphere that is downright luxurious.

Seats are soft, too. as befits cushions that are instantly convertible into twin beds. And roomy! "It's like a rolling hotel," Red declares. These were, in fact, the widest seats in the industry, in 1956, providing four-and-a-half more inches of front hip room than that year's Mercury, five inches more rear shoulder room than the Olds 88. The Hudson stands three-quarters of an inch lower than a 1956 Cadillac, yet its front and rear head room, respectively, are an inch-and-three-quarters and nine-tenths of an inch greater. In short, like

The Diminishing Fortunes of the Four Great Independents

The post-World War II era brought a period of great prosperity to the automobile industry, and especially to the embattled independent producers. But in a sense it was a Fool's Paradise. Watching his company's ledgers, Nash-Kelvinator president George Mason saw that rapidly escalating tooling costs were pushing his company's (and everyone else's) break-even point even higher.

The answer, Mason could see, lay in the consolidation of the four major independent manufacturers, spreading those tooling costs over a broader base. But his competitors, complacent in their newfound prosperity, failed to see the logic in his argument.

The result may be seen in the accompanying chart. The smaller firms were forced to stay with a given body design more than twice as long, on the average, as their larger com-petitors. And in an era of rapid change in fashions, their cars began to look dated.

And so, both sales and market share began to fall—not to speak of what happened to profits. A part of George Mason's dream came true shortly before his death in 1954, with the formation of American Motors through the merger of Hudson with Nash-Kelvinator. But although AMC's Rambler was to prosper mightily for a time, that merger—in comparison to what might have been—was too little, too late.

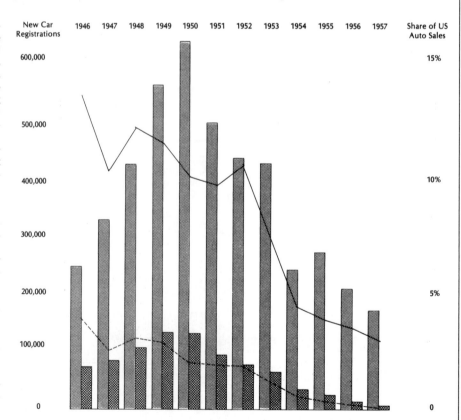

Legend: Taller bars show combined new car registrations, Hudson, Nash, Stude, Packard. Short bars show new car registrations, Hudson only (Rambler excluded). Solid line shows percent of market held by four independents. Broken line shows percent of market held by Hudson (Rambler excluded).

specifications

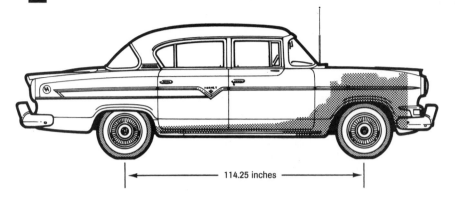

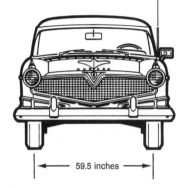

114.25 inches

59.5 inches

1956 Hudson Hornet Special

Original price	$2,626 f.o.b. factory, including federal excise tax.
Options on dR car	Air conditioning; twin beds; overdrive; radio with dual speakers; left outside rearview mirror; wheel covers; white sidewall tires; two-tone paint.

ENGINE

Type	V-8, overhead valves with hydraulic lifters.
Bore x stroke	3.5 inches x 3.25 inches.
Displacement	250.0 cubic inches.
Max bhp @ rpm	190 @ 4,900.
Max torque @ rpm	240 @ 2,000-3,000.
Compression ratio	8.0:1.
Induction system	Carter WGD 2-bbl carburetor, model 2352S.
Lubrication system	Full pressure.
Exhaust system	Single.
Electrical system	12-volt.

CLUTCH

Type	Single dry plate.
Diameter	10 inches.
Actuation	Mechanical, foot pedal.

TRANSMISSION

Type	3-speed, synchronized 2nd and 3rd gears; overdrive.
Ratios: 1st	2.57:1.
2nd	1.55:1.
3rd	1.00:1.
Overdrive	0.70:1.
Reverse	3.49:1.

DIFFERENTIAL

Type	Hypoid.
Ratio	4.55:1.
Drive axles	Semi-floating.

STEERING

Make/type	Gemmer worm-and-roller.
Turns lock-to-lock	4.5.
Ratio	20.0:1 (gear), 26.0:1 (overall).
Turning radius	39' 3".

BRAKES

Type	4-wheel hydraulic, drum type.
Drum diameter	10 inches.
Total swept area	158.9 square inches.

CHASSIS & BODY

Frame and body	All-steel, unitized.
Body style	4-door sedan.

SUSPENSION

Front	Independent, coil springs.
Rear	Coil springs, solid axle.
Tires	6.70 x 15.
Wheels	Steel disc.

WEIGHTS AND MEASURES

Wheelbase	114.25 inches.
Overall length	202.25 inches.
Overall width	78 inches.
Overall height	78 inches.
Front tread	59.5 inches.
Rear track	59.6875 inches.
Ground clearance	7.5 inches.
Shipping weight	3,467 pounds with standard equipment; 3,630 as equipped.

CAPACITIES

Crankcase	5 quarts (6 with filter)
Cooling system	22 quarts (with heater)
Fuel tank	20 gallons

PRODUCTION

'56 Hudson	10,671 (excluding Ramblers)
This model & body style	1,528

PERFORMANCE

Acceleration (standing start)	
0-30 mph	4.6 seconds.
0-45 mph	8.5 seconds.
0-60 mph	14.6 seconds.
Quarter mile	19.7 seconds; 69.7 mph
Top speed: fastest run	102.1 mph.
Slowest run	98.8 mph.
Average (4 runs)	101.5 mph.
Stopping distance	151 feet from 60 mph.

From *Motor Trend*, July 1956

the Nash from which it was derived, this car was built for roominess and comfort.

The dashboard cluster, placed squarely in front of the driver, includes instruments to measure the fuel supply and to indicate the engine temperature. But idiot lights—pioneered by Hudson back in the mid-thirties—are used in place of ampere and oil pressure gauges.

There are some nice touches which we can appreciate. The hood release is in the driver's compartment where it belongs, not out front, where it would invite the theft of one's battery. A drawer in the center of the dash takes the place of the customary glove box. No more fumbling about for items that fall out when the door is opened. (What ever

Another Visit With George Romney

Twice in recent years *Special Interest Autos* has been privileged to interview George Romney, president of American Motors Corporation at the time our driveReport car was built.

It was Romney, of course, who was responsible for boosting the Rambler into fourth place in US auto sales before he resigned to become governor of Michigan, and later Secretary of Housing and Urban Development. And it was Romney, too, who made the decision to "kill off" both Nash and Hudson at the conclusion of the 1957 model year.

In our last discussion (see *SIA* #66) Governor Romney told us that studies he had made while he was an official of the Automobile Manufacturers Association clearly showed that the average automobile trip was no more than 13 miles in length. "That meant," he said, "that this idea that you had to have a car for transcontinental travel just wasn't basically correct. People needed a vehicle for short trips."

So George Romney was, and is, a true believer in the small car concept. And yet, in taking over the presidency of American Motors upon the death of its founder, George Mason, Romney found himself at the head of a concern that was deeply involved in the manufacture of big cars—as well as of the compact Rambler.

How, we wondered, did the full-sized cars fit into the picture as he saw it, that day in October 1954 when he first took command at AMC?

So we asked him.

SIA: At the time of the AMC merger, Governor, what were the plans for the full-sized Hudsons and Nashes?

Romney: The plan was to consolidate the manufacture of the two cars, in the interest of economy. And to consolidate the tooling, to the extent that was possible.

SIA: For the long haul, was a new body shell in the works, possibly based on that attractive prototype built for Nash by Pinin Farina?

Romney: Well, that was one of the first major decisions I had to make: whether to continue those big cars, or whether to drop them. And of course I made the decision to drop them and sink or swim with the Rambler.

SIA: When was that decision made?

Romney: Oh, I'd have to go back and check

it. But it was certainly made by '56, because if we were going to continue the big cars we'd have to get right at the problem of design and tooling and so on.

SIA: We note that the various Hudson series were priced a few dollars higher than their Nash counterparts. Does this indicate a move toward establishing Hudson as the upper medium-priced line, with Nash priced a little below it?

Romney: Oh, it was just a way of dealing with the situation at that time. Because really, there was no decision to go ahead and tool up separate Nash and Hudson models. There may have been some minor differences that accounted for the price spread, I don't recall. We may have had a little more tooling on the Hudson, to make the basic Nash body look different for the Hudson.

SIA: What about the dealer organizations? Was it in your thinking—initially, that is—to keep the Nash and Hudson dealers separate, or to combine them?

Romney: Well, initially.... Look, the difference between Mason and me was this:

Mason might well have undertaken to perpetuate the Nash and the Hudson. Because I think he thought of the Rambler as a supplementary vehicle. I concluded very early that the Rambler was the car of the future, and I wasn't thinking in terms of perpetuating two separate organizations, two separate lines of cars in Nash and Hudson. I reached that decision fairly early after I took over.

SIA: Now, if Packard had become part of the merger, presumably making more capital available, how would that have affected your thinking?

Romney: Well, then we would have undertaken to tool big cars and perpetuate them. But the impossibility of the Packard merger became apparent right after I took over. [Packard president James J.] Nance made it very clear by moves that he made that he thought he was going to take over American Motors. He talked about me as a fellow who just carried Mason's briefcase; I didn't know much about the business, and so on. He even told some magazine people that he would be taking over American Motors by the first of 1955!

We had reciprocal agreements with respect to Packard's purchase of stampings from us, and our purchase of V-8 engines from them.

But he acquired the Briggs stamping plant and I knew from that, he wasn't going to go through with the reciprocal understanding that had been reached with Mason.

So I knew very early that the Packard thing was through.

SIA: Speaking of engines, was the AMC V-8 something that Nash had been developing prior to the merger?

Romney: Yes, we had started it before the merger, but we didn't have it ready by '55. And if we had been able to work out the reciprocal deal with Packard, we probably wouldn't have gone ahead with our own V-8—although we were working on it.

SIA: That engine was intended for use in both the Rambler and the big cars?

Romney: Yes, that's right.

SIA: Nash was about five years behind most of the industry in developing that V-8. How come? Was it a matter of development costs?

Romney: Well, tooling costs. After all, the reason for the merger was the heavy burden of tooling costs on a relatively low volume. And of course that was also the reason for talking with Packard about a reciprocal arrangement.

SIA: So it was just the economics of the situation that caused Nash's—and AMC's—delay in getting into the V-8 thing?

Romney: That's exactly right.

SIA: One final question, Governor. In your view, when did Hudson and Nash pass the point of no return? That is, when did their demise become inevitable?

Romney: Just as soon as I made the decision to drop them. As things worked out, that was within the first year after I took over.

And there you have it. Our driveReport car was doomed before it was ever built!

But Governor Romney's comments prompt us to speculate: What if Packard had become a part of American Motors? Might Packard, Hudson and Nash all have survived? How might their cars have looked, say, by 1957 or '58? How might a new body shell, perhaps patterned after Nash's Pinin Farina prototype, have been adapted to Hudson's and—especially—Packard's styling traditions?

Time was to prove the soundness of George Romney's judgment in putting all his chips on the Rambler. But one can't help thinking about what might have been....

1956 HUDSON

happened to *that* feature, Detroit? It's a good one!) And the radio has twin speakers, one at either end of the dashboard.

Unlike the Nash, with its traditional clutch-pedal starter, this near-twin from Hudson is fired by a twist of the ignition key. And promptly! The engine, with its zero-lash hydraulic lifters, is whisper-quiet at idle.

The clutch, which Red recently replaced, is smooth. Shifts are easy; the linkage works better than we expected of a column-mounted mechanism. Ac-

A proper motoring cap is necessary for piloting such an unusual and distinctive car.

celeration, while hardly neck-snapping, is more than adequate.

Steering, which is non-powered, is unexpectedly light and easy, but disconcertingly slow. The Hudson heels over at an uncomfortable angle when it's pushed hard through the turns, yet it's easy to maintain control.

Unlike the larger Hornets, the Special does not employ Hudson's famed dual braking system, in which mechanical linkage is provided in the event of hydraulic failure. But the binders are excellent nevertheless. With minimal pedal pressure (though they are not power-assisted), they bring the car to

rest promptly, smoothly, in a straight line—and with less nosedive than we had anticipated.

Visibility is marvelous. Hudson and Nash had the widest windshields in the business in 1956. And while the glass is shaped in "dogleg" fashion, we didn't bump our knees on the corner, as we've done with some GM cars of that era. Nor was the distortion in the compound-curved glass bad enough to cause any problems.

The window cranks furnished another surprise. They work easily and fast, only two full turns being sufficient to raise or lower the windows all the way.

Red Burke, riding with us in the Hudson's back seat, expressed disgust with one facet of the car's performance. As we pushed repeatedly through hard turns while Jim Tanji fired his camera for the action shots, one hubcap kept flying off. Red told us he had a new-old-stock wheel cover in his garage, and we'll bet it was installed not long after he got home.

One of the more felicitous pieces of equipment on the Burke car is its AMC air-conditioner. Originally introduced on the 1954 Nash, this was the first of the single-unit automotive air-conditioners—far less expensive than the competition's equipment in those days, and at least as effective as any on the market. Integral with the heater, it takes in fresh air at the cowl, filters it, heats or cools it to the desired temperature, and circulates it throughout the car. "The cool air just surrounds you," Red observes, adding that it is "one of the most satisfactory air-conditioners I've ever used."

We didn't buy a new car in 1956, and in all honesty, if we had it wouldn't have been a Hudson. Nor, in retrospect, would it necessarily be our first choice today. And yet, we came away from the half-day we spent with Red Burke's car with a healthy respect for the hybrid Hudson. It's a well-built automobile that is exceptionally roomy and comfortable, more than adequate in its performance, easy to drive, and economical to operate.

Perhaps it deserved more consideration than it got from the motoring public of 1956. ⚙

Acknowledgments and Bibliography
Automotive Industries, *January 15, 1956; March 15, 1956; April 15,1956; John Conde,* The Cars That Hudson Built; Standard Catalog of American Cars; *Jerry Heasley,* The Production Figure Book for US Cars; *Factory sales literature; Hudson owners manual, 1956; Jim Lodge, "Nash and Hudson Special V-8 Road Test,"* Motor Trend, *July 1956.*

Our thanks to Bob Aaron, Hubbard, Ohio; Tom and Lynn Burke, Concord, California; Ralph Dunwoodie, Sun Valley, Nevada; D.J Kava, Beaumont, Texas; Joe Patton, Fort Bragg, California. Special thanks to Red and Edna Burke, Fort Bragg, California.

The Rise And Fall Of The Postwar Hudson

Hudson had not been treated kindly in the dozen or so years that preceded World War II. The Depression had been rough on the entire industry, of course, but even 1940 and '41, very good years for most of its competitors, found Hudson's production running at only about 27 percent of the company's record 1929 total.

But the postwar period gave Hudson, along with the rest of the industry, a fresh start. Production was limited at first by the company's allocations of sheet steel and other critical materials, but by 1948—the year Hudson introduced its sensational "step-down" design—that problem had eased. The rapid rise and the precipitous fall that followed can be seen in the following table of Hudson's production*, 1946-1957.

Year	Production
1946	95,000
1947	95,000
1948	117,200
1949	159,100
1950	121,408
1951	131,915
1952	70,000
1953	66,143
1954	50,660
1955	10,321
1956	10,671
1957	3,876

*Model years, Rambler excluded

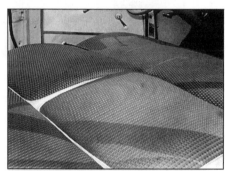

Top: *It's a high, wide, and very comfortable car.* **Center left:** *Centrally placed bin can carry lots of gloves.* **Center right:** *Hudson also inherited Nash's famous bed/seats.* **Above:** *Room to spare in capacious trunk.*

BLUEPRINTS

'46 and '47 Hudsons
by Bob Hovorka

YOU didn't have to step down to get into these Hudsons, and there weren't any sills to trip over getting out. Although they were taller than most of today's sport utilities, they rode smoothly, handled well, and were built as solid as the proverbial masonry lavatory. Long overshadowed by Hudson's race-winning "Step-downs," the oft-underrated '46 and '47 models suffered from that "warmed-over pre-war car" syndrome.

Sure they were, but that didn't make them poor performers. With a long history of building quick cars, Hudson's penchant for record breaking continued up to the start of World War II. At the time, Hudson held over 120 AAA records. Those "warmed-over" '46s and '47s came from the same stock.

Powered by either a 212-cubic-inch side-valve six, or a 254-cubic-inch side-valve eight, the big 121-inch-wheelbase cars weren't the quickest off the line. But with engine blocks cast of high quality chromium alloy steel, and pistons spinning forged cranks and rods, there wasn't a highway built that either engine couldn't traverse day in and day out at posted speeds PLUS! Features like Silicon steel intake, and Silichrome

steel exhaust valves, coupled with piston rings that were pinned to prevent unwanted rotation, gave Hudson "more *official* performance and endurance records than are held by any other stock car in the world."

A lengthy list of safety features went along with its performance records. Long before government-mandated dual braking systems, Hudsons featured a reserve mechanical backup system that automatically took over in case of hydraulic failure. Chassis side members were deep box section affairs with a huge "X" member supplementing five cross members. Bolted to this frame was a semi-unit body with "floor, quarter panels, front end and roof panel welded together to insure maximum strength and rigidity.... Under foot, over head, all around you in a Hudson, are exclusive features that have given it the title of America's Safest Car."

Driving one of these large, non-power-assisted vehicles is not as difficult as might be expected. Instead of the usual unequal drag link setup, true "Center-Point Steering" operated from the exact center of the car, giving excellent road feel and ease of control. Coupled with a steering wheel that would look more at

home in a Mack truck, the car is easily maneuvered through most situations. Facing a dashboard filled with gold and chrome glitter, the Hudson driver turns the ignition key, touches a large plastic button marked "S" and either engine springs to life. An easy push on Hudson's oil-filled clutch (which, depending on engine, had either 90 or 108 corks that gave a cushioning effect during engagement) and you were on your way. Shifts were exceptionally smooth, the wet clutch turning even a novice stick shifter into an expert. Sitting on seats whose leather and fabric quality belied its $1,500 to $2,200 price tag, there's a feeling of substance and elegance that's practically non-existent today.

Never content to follow the crowd, Hudson built cars its own way. From overbuilt bodies and frames, to splash-lubricated engines, they stood apart. The indented grille became a haven for amber-colored fog lights — and that radio — the one which allowed the driver to change volume or station from a foot-operated pedal without ever taking his eyes off the road.... Well, it too showed Hudson's free thinking. Warmed over pre-war? Maybe! Excellent value? Always! 🏁

BLUEPRINTS

1954 Hudson
by Bob Hovorka

The name lingered until 1957, but they really stopped building Hudson Motor Cars in 1954. Even then, they were six-year-old slope-back sixes, in an era of square-back V-8s. And while today's "full-size" Chevrolet may look suspiciously similar to its 1977 "down-size" counterpart, back in the fifties you couldn't keep a body ten years and survive.

To be honest, Hudson's 308-cubic-inch six was antiquated the day it was introduced. Oh, Rambler, Plymouth, Pontiac, and a few others still offered flathead sixes in 1954, but they were aimed at economy conscious buyers. Hudson was crowing performance — and when the new Hornet six hit the showrooms in 1951, performance was spelled V-8.... Usually Olds Rocket or Chrysler FirePower. Hudson had to he kidding!

Well, Hudson may have been a lot of things; kidding wasn't one of them. Combined with the ground-hugging step-down body, that obsolete flathead six ruled NASCAR and AAA circuits for three-and-a-half years. Even in 1954, when Buick's "Hot" Century was the darling of magazine road testers, and Chrysler's 235-hp Hemi topped Detroit's power pillar, Hudson brochures stated: "Hudson now holds *every* AAA competitive stock-car record and the National Stock-Car Championship in three major racing associations."

Hudson offered safety and handling features no other car could match. Hudson's unique "Monobilt body-and-frame" allowed Hudson engineers to drop the floor between the frame rails. When introduced, it had "the lowest center of gravity in any American stock car." So low you had to "Step-down" to get in. From a safety standpoint, "Rugged, box-section steel girders completely encircle the passenger compartment — and even extend outside the rear wheels." This, coupled with front and rear stabilizer bars and splayed rear springs, gave Hudson step-downs unmatched stability whether negotiating a curvy stretch of highway or high-speed race course.

Added to this were Hudson's exclusive Triple-Safe brakes, "a reserve mechanical brake system, ready to take over automatically from the same brake pedal if hydraulic pressure should fail." *Safety Engineering* voted Hudson's step-down "America's Safest Car." For two straight years the American Society of Engineers gave Hudson "the most advanced ideas in design" award. But back in the fifties safety didn't sell cars; yearly styling changes did. And that was one area where the Monobilt body was a liability.

By 1954 the hump-back Hudsons were considered old fashioned. Because the girder-like framework was such an integral part of the Monobilt body, major styling changes were engineering headaches and accounting nightmares. Yet Hudson gave it one last try. They threw off the softness of earlier step-downs and tightened the body lines. A single straight grille bar replaced the old down turned version; Hudson's traditional lighted triangle still occupied a prominent spot. A new functional air scoop visually lowered the high-domed hood, and up top a one-piece windshield finally arrived. But the back end was the real surprise. The rounded bustle disappeared. Straight line fenders lifted the rear — ending in a pair of triangular shaped taillights. They gave coupes, hardtops, and convertibles a fresh contemporary look, but they couldn't disguise the old torpedo-back of the bread and butter sedans.

All in all, it was a tremendous accomplishment for the ailing old company. If it only could have happened three years earlier. ☙

Hudson Model Year Production, 1909-1957

Year	Production Totals
1909	1,000+*
1910	4,556
1911	6,486
1912	5,708
1913	6,404
1914	10,261
1915	12,864
1916	25,772
1917	20,976
1918	12,526
1919	18,175
1920	22,268
1921	13,721
1922	28,242
1923	46,337
1924	59,427
1925	109,840
1926	70,261
1927	66,034
1928	52,316
1929	71,179
1930	36,674
1931	17,487
1932	7,777
1933	2,401
1934	27,130

Year	Production Totals
1935	29,476
1936	25,409
1937	19,848
1938	51,078
1939	82,161
1940	87,900
1941	79,529
1942	40,661
1946	91,626
1947	92,083
1948	117,200
1949	**159,100*****
1950	121,400
1951	131,910
1952	70,000
1953	66,143
1954	50,687**
1955	20,321**
1956	10,671**
1957	3,108

* No precise first-year production records are available

** Total does not include Metropolitan or Rambler series

*** Hudson's biggest year ever

Hudson Engine Specifications: 1910-1957

Year	Cylinders.	Displacement. (cubic inches)	Bore x Stroke	Output (gross horsepower)
1910-11	Inline-4	198.8	3.750 x 4.500	20
1911-12	I-4	226	4.000 x 4.500	33
1913	I-4	280.6	4.125 x 5.250	37
1913-15	I-6	421	4.125 x 5.250	54
1914-16	I-6	288.5	3.500 x 5.000	42
1916-26	I-6	289	3.500 x 5.000	76
1927-29	I-6	288.5	3.500 x 5.000	92
1930	I-8	213.8	2.750 x 4.500	80
1931	I-8	233.7	2.875 x 4.500	87
1932	I-8	254.4	3.000 x 4.500	101
1933	I-8	254.4	3.000 x 4.500	101/110
1933	I-6	193.1	2.937 x 4.750	73/80
1934	I-8	254.4	3.000 x 4.500	108/113/121
1935-36	I-8	254.4	3.000 x 4.500	113/124
1935-36	I-6	212	3.000 x 5.000	93/100
1937-39	I-8	254.4	3.000 x 4.500	122
1937	I-6	212	3.000 x 5.000	101/107
1938	I-6	212	3.000 x 5.000	83/101/107
1939	I-6	212	3.000 x 5.000	86/96/101
1940-42	I-8	254.4	3.000 x 4.500	128
1940-42	I-6	175	3.000 x 4.125	92
1940-42	I-6	212	3.000 x 5.000	102
1946-52	I-8	254.4	3.000 x 4.500	128
1946-47	I-6	212	3.000 x 5.000	103
1948-49	I-6	262	3.562 x 4.375	121
1950-53	I-6	232	3.562 x 3.875	112
1950-51	I-6	262	3.562 x 4.375	123
1951-53	I-6	308	3.812 x 4.500	145
1952-53	I-6	262	3.562 x 4.375	127
1953-54	I-6	202	3.000 x 4.750	104
1954	I-6	232	3.562 x 3.875	126
1954	I-6	262	3.562 x 4.375	140
1954-55	I-6	308	3.812 x 4.500	160
1954	I-6	202	3.000 x 4.750	114
1955	I-6	195.6	3.125 x 4.250	90
1955-56	I-6	202	3.000 x 4.750	120
1955	V-8	320	3.812 x 3.500	208
1956	I-6	202	3.000 x 4.750	130
1956	I-6	308	3.812 x 4.500	165/175
1956	V-8	352	4.000 x 3.500	220
1956	V-8	250	3.500 x 3.250	190
1957	V-8	327	4.000 x 3.250	255

Other Hudson Books

History of Hudson, Don Butler, Crestline Publishing

Cars that Hudson Built, John Conde, Arnold-Porter Publishing,

Hudson, the Classic Post War Years, Richard Langworth

Hudson 1946-1957, R.M. Clarke

Hudson Clubs & Specialists

For a complete list of all regional Hudson clubs and national clubs' chapters, visit **Car Club Central** at **www.hemmings.com**. With nearly 10,000 car clubs listed, it's the largest car club site in the world! Not wired? For the most up-to-date information, consult the latest issue of *Hemmings Motor News* and/or *Hemmings' Collector Car Almanac*. Call toll free, 1-800-CAR-HERE, Ext. 550.

HUDSON CLUB

Hudson-Essex-Terraplane Club
PO Box 715
Milford, IN 46542-0715
(43 regional chapters, 7 international chapters)

Other Important Clubs

Antique Automobile Club of America
501 W. Governor Road
Hershey, PA 17033
717-534-1910
(311 regional chapters, 7 international chapters)

Horseless Carriage Club of America
3311 Fairhaven Dr.
Orange, CA 92866-1357
661-326-1023
(91 regional chapters, 7 international chapters)

Veteran Motor Car Club of America
4441 W. Altadena Ave.
Glendale, AZ 85304-3526
800-428-7327
(82 regional chapters)

HUDSON SPECIALISTS

Bastian Automotive Restoration
4170 Finch Ave.
Fairfield, OH 45014
513-738-4268
Restoration, repair, and rewiring

Guild of Automotive Restorers
P.O. Box 1150, 44 Bridge St.
Bradford, ON Canada L3Z 2B5
905-775-0499
Restorations and sales

Hibernia Auto Restorations Inc
52 Maple Terrace
Hibernia, NJ 07842
973-627-1882
Collectible car restorations.

Hudson Motor Car Co Memorabilia
Ken Poynter
19638 Huntington
Harper Woods, MI 48225
313-886-9292
Anything pertaining to Hudson

K-GAP Automotive Parts
P.O. Box 3065
Santa Fe Springs, CA 90670
714-523-0403
Reproduction parts & accessories

Kanter Auto Products
76 Monroe St.
Booton, NJ 07005
800-526-1096
Parts and literature

Old Coach Works Restoration Inc.
1206 Badger St.
Yorkville, IL 60560-1701
630-553-0414
Complete and partial restorations

Garth B Peterson
122 N. Conklin Rd.
Veradale, WA 99037
509-926-4620
NOS and used parts

Pilgrim's Auto Restorations
3888 Hill Road
Lakeport, CA 95453
707-262-1062
Restoration, body and paint

Don Robertson
2411 Gardner St.
Elliston, VA 24087
540-268-2837
Hudson cars and parts

Tom Taylor
P.O. Box 129
Guinda, CA 95637
530-796-4106
NOS parts

Vintage Auto Parts Inc.
24300 Hwy. 9
Woodinville, WA 98072
800-426-5911
NOS and used parts

Webb's Classic Auto Parts
5084 W. State Rd. 114
Huntington, IN 46750
219-344-1714
Rambler parts, Hudson literature

Wenner's
5449 Tannery Rd.
Schnecksville, PA 18078
610-799-5419
Rambler parts

White Post Restorations
One Old Car Dr., P.O. Drawer D
White Post, VA 22663
540-8371140
Complete and partial restorations

Notes